Banana Thinking

Creative and Innovative Concepts
for Personal Effectiveness

by
Mick Harrison

Trade Life Books
Tulsa, Oklahoma

Banana Thinking
Creative and Innovative Concepts for
Personal Effectiveness

ISBN 1-57757-000-6

Copyright © 1996 by Michael D. Harrison

Published by TRADE LIFE BOOKS
P. O. Box 55325
Tulsa, Oklahoma 74155

Illustrations by Cory Edwards

Banana Endorsements

"'Banana Thinking' has some strong ideas to contribute."

Eddie Albert

"I had the opportunity to read... 'Banana Thinking' on a flight from Memphis to Philadelphia. I was so impressed that I bought copies for all of our employees. It has proven to be a great addition to our TQM effort."

Bob Trenner, President
TREND Instruments Inc.

"This little book packs a powerful punch. I couldn't put it down. If you are a manager interested in stretching your thinking in order to become more efficient or add more value to your product, reading this book is a sure-fire way to achieve your goal."

Rod Mabry, Dean
College of Business
Administration
University of Tulsa

Banana Perusal

"Thanks for the copy of your book and for your warm letter: it was good of you to take the time and trouble to get them to me. I've put your book on my reading stack where I can give it a better read than the perusal I've just enjoyed. I wish you well with it as with all else."

Charlton Heston

Banana Unendorsements

"Thank you so much for thinking of Jimmy Dean as an endorser of your book 'Banana Thinking.' Mr. Dean did indeed scan the book and enjoyed it very much. However, he asked me to tell you that he does not indulge in endorsements of any kind except for Jimmy Dean Sausage!"

Mary H. Moore
Executive Assistant to
Jimmy Dean

"Miss Hepburn asked me to thank you for thinking of her – but she is bogged down with other projects and cannot add another to her already long list of commitments – Good luck to you."

Sharon Powers
for Miss Hepburn

"Thank you for your letter and the enclosed copy of your book, 'Banana Thinking.' Unfortunately, Ms. Day cannot even consider endorsing your book, as a policy has been adopted not to endorse any specific products, in order not to favor one product over another. However, we thank you for your kind request and wish you much success with your book."

Ria Rosenberg
for Ms. Day

"Mr. Douglas thanks you for sending him the book. Unfortunately, he is prohibited by his agent to make an endorsement, but he wishes you much success."

Lorraine McManus
Assistant to Kirk Douglas

"Thank you for inviting me to write an endorsement to your book. As you can appreciate, I receive many such requests, but unfortunately, time does not permit me to honor most of them. Although I must decline, I wish you much success with 'Banana Thinking.'"

Lee A. Iacocca

"Just a note to let you know that your letter and book, 'Banana Thinking,' arrived safely in Mr. Hope's office. I know he'll appreciate your letter and thoughtfulness. Thank you for thinking of Mr. Hope and for taking the time to write."

Marie Boren
Secretary to Bob Hope

"Thank you for your letter dated February 20, a copy of your book BANANA THINKING, both sent to Pat Boone for his attention. We do wish you well with your book – unfortunately, we have recently adopted a policy of cutting back tremendously on endorsing books – due to the fact that Pat receives requests every day to endorse someone's book or product, and in all fairness, we cannot accept every request."

Maureen Mata (Mrs)
Admin. Assistant to
Pat Boone

"Thank you for your letter and the book, 'Banana Thinking' as a gift to Richard Petty. He is honored you would want him to endorse your book, but he must decline. Hopefully he is able to read the book during some leisure time, but the racing schedule is so busy at this time and he is away during most of this time. Thank you again for your consideration."

Martha Jane Bonkemeyer
Secretary to Richard Petty

Contents

Contents

"I could carve a better man out of a banana."

Theodore Roosevelt

Introduction

This is a book about personal effectiveness, motivation, idea generation, living life to the fullest, and being a good neighbor. It was written for people who dare to break out of the box, for thinkers and innovators living and working in an ever-changing world. If you want to improve yourself and your environment, this book is for you.

You will read much about work in the following pages because that is where we spend most of our time. It is important to balance the time we spend on the job with our personal activities and to put both of these aspects of our lives in perspective with the rest of the world. Work is the primary way in which we contribute to society; therefore, our on-the-job performance is very important. But of equal importance is the manner in which we play and enjoy our lives.

It is my sincere hope that after reading this book you will understand your existence a little better and will learn to accept the differences that life offers. I also hope you will gain new insight to the world in which you live, work and play.

The Author

PART I

Banana Facts of Life

CHAPTER 1

Banana Thinking

Otto awoke early in the jungle thicket that he fondly knew as home. With a powerful thrust from his long arms he stood erect, then in a commanding voice uttered his first sounds of the day, "UHH – UHH! OOH! OOH! OOH! RIHH! RIHH!"

Otto was hungry, and so were the rest of his clan. He and the fourteen other gorillas in his family lived comfortably in an area of the jungle that abounded in banana trees. After their morning stretch and some authoritative chest pounding, they set out to vanquish every banana that lay in their path.

The gorillas spied their objective, a gangly growth with big, green leaves and bunches of golden bananas just waiting to be eaten. Otto was the first to arrive at the banana tree, so he swiftly reached up to pick the first prize of the day. With two quick swipes he peels the banana, and the world as we know it will never be the same.

So what is it, you may ask, that makes Otto's banana eating episode different from any other? The answer and the "root" of banana thinking lies in this article published in the July 1992 issue of *Quality Digest*.

*"Learning a new way to peel a banana should
show that unlimited possibilities await discovery."*

"Banana Thinking"[1]

A work associate came into my office during lunch time the other day eating a banana. It wasn't a terribly significant event except for one aspect. He was eating the banana peeled from the bottom instead of the stem end. I told him that I had never thought of peeling a banana in such a manner. His response was that it was much easier to peel a banana from the bottom than from the top. I could hardly believe that I had never thought of peeling a banana from the bottom.

My buddy told me that he had recently seen a TV documentary on gorillas. As the story was told, a family of gorillas surrounded a banana tree. The gorillas peeled bananas from the bottom as fast as they could so that each gorilla could eat as many as possible. Then they went on to eat the banana tree itself. We should take a lesson from the expert banana eaters. But we should stop short of consuming the whole banana tree.

I assume that when I was much younger someone showed me how to peel a banana from the stem end and I never questioned that knowledge. It is very likely that it was my mother or father who first showed me how to peel a banana. I am also very certain that the idea of there being only one way to peel a banana is connected to the concept that we rarely question our parent's teachings. So with this thought in mind I made a special effort to show my son how to peel a banana from the bottom and the top with the hope of sparking his imagination in other areas.

Many of us insist on carrying our limited thinking to the grave. Somehow we choose to quit learning early in life when there is a lifetime of things still to learn. Learning a new way to peel a banana should show that unlimited possibilities await discovery.

Before I was introduced to the *way of the banana*, I would sometimes resort to cutting below the stem to get to the fruit without bruising it. I would do this primarily when the banana was a little green. But now I have the knowledge to peel those green bananas as easily as the ripe ones.

> *Many of us insist on carrying our limited thinking to the grave.*

Here was something so simple – peeling a banana, and I never questioned there was a more effective way to get to the fruit. Upon seeing the documentary on gorillas, what I heard from my work associate was verified before my eyes. I was fascinated. From then on it was only natural to presume there must be a host of other similar situations where I could apply the banana concept. It was suddenly clear to me that there must be different ways to peel other fruits, too, and there must be different ways to solve those simple problems that I encountered every day.

So I began to look for innovative ways to do the simplest tasks and make basic decisions. I discovered the banana concept could be related to almost everything I do, and that looking at things from the bottom and the top gave me a new view of most situations. I began peeling away at my old way of thinking trying to come up with the non-traditional approach to the most basic tasks. And I began looking for effectiveness as I searched for new ideas.

I always thought of myself as an innovator, but the banana incident showed me that I was just as guilty of confining my thinking to conventional wisdom as the next guy. I scrutinized the people around me, pondering how often a truly original idea is formed by anyone today. I even questioned whether we have possibly come to the point that nothing we do is original.

I began searching through most of the basic concepts that deal with truly original thinking. I looked long and hard. Then I found it – a simple, but profound notion: "Imagination is more important than knowledge." And who coined such a preposterous idea? Albert Einstein was his name, and thinking was his game. Einstein was truly the most original thinker of our time.

With this notion in mind, I set out in search of my own original idea, and after awhile, I actually had one. The thought I developed was really a corollary to Einstein's quote, but original nevertheless. "The majority of people have stopped coming up with new ideas because they have stopped imagining."

Coming up with new ideas is not as complicated as you may think. There are only a few basic things that you need to know to be successful. One of them is to keep learning about the world in which you live and strive. And if you can learn something new about peeling a banana, you can only imagine the endless possibilities there are to improve the very nature of how you think, work, and make decisions.

In fact, there are new ways to do what you have done the same all of your life. There are new ways to get out of bed in the morning, and there are better routes to travel to work. There are new ways to shop for groceries, and new ways to prepare them. There are new ways to communicate with your work associates, and there are countless ways to improve your listening skills. There are new ways to word process, and there are many new ways to electronically manage data. In short, there are new ways to think and new methods to generate ideas. There are millions of books to read and endless knowledge to acquire. And all you have to do is to be open to the way of the banana.

The majority of people have stopped coming up with new ideas because they have stopped imagining.

Go peel a banana from the bottom, and you will see. You will discover a new concept that can help you take an innovative look at everything you do. You will become a more effective thinker. You will become a better banana thinking you.

The Bottom Banana Peeler's Creed

A banana is good,
It can show you something new;
You will soon have new ideas,
And you will find out something true.

It can show you something now,
It can show you something then;
It can even change the minds,
Of limited thinking men.

So peel it from the bottom,
And do it every day;
You will be inspired,
With this more effective way.

CHAPTER 2

Apples Too!

"**U**HH – UHH – UHH – RIHH – RIHH – RIHH – ERRA – ERRA!" Otto says bananas are best, but apples are good too!

"Apples Too!"[1]

The other day I was sharing the banana thinking concept with a good friend, and he told me a wonderful story about his three-year-old daughter. He said that he recently summoned her to the kitchen, gave her an apple, then sent her on her way. When she returned later without the apple, he asked her what she had done with it and she said that it had been eaten. Then he asked a second question, "What did you do with the core of the apple, honey?" And when she answered, he was astonished. "What core?" she asked. Apparently the girl, having never eaten an apple before, without instruction, decided to eat the whole apple – including the core. Upon hearing this tale of "self-direction," I was overwhelmed and began examining additional banana ideas.

Gorillas don't eat apples on a regular basis. I suppose it is because apples are not available in most regions where they forage for food. But, I wonder if they could show us a better way to eat apples too?

23

Do you suppose it is instinct that paved the way for bottom banana peeling, or was it just gravity? The first thing a gorilla sees when looking at a banana tree is a bunch of bananas with the stem ends facing down, and the black buttons on the bottoms of the bananas facing up. This is the way they grow, with what we call the "top" of the banana closest to the ground. Therefore, when a gorilla picks a banana from a tree, he holds it so that the bottom is up, and the stem end is facing down.

A Matter of Apples or Bananas

One could argue that gorillas are merely taking the shortest route to the banana fruit by peeling from the bottom. But we should give the gorillas a little more credit for their brilliant discovery. Let's compare it to the kind of effectiveness that comes from performing a similar task over and over again. Just imagine that you ate ten thousand bananas a year. Wouldn't you have discovered the most effective way to peel a banana long before reading about it in a book? Sure you would, and that is what the gorillas have done. Bananas being their staple food, they have simply had the opportunity to eat around bad habits and have come up with the most effective way to get to the fruit.

Therefore, it is my assertion that if gorillas ate apples on a daily basis, they would probably show us a new twist. Look at horses, they eat the whole apple. A horse doesn't care that the core isn't quite as tasty as the rest of the fruit. He pulverizes the spheroid into mush with a few movements of his extraordinary jaws. Wow!

That reminds me of a related story. I met a friend at the tennis court the other day, and he had just finished eating an apple, or so I thought. The core was in his hand, and he had clearly eaten all of the white pulpy fruit. As we were walking to our court, to my astonishment, my friend simply popped the core of the apple into his mouth, chewed it thoroughly, and swallowed it. My first question was, "What about the seeds?" Then I explained how when I was in grade school someone told me they were poisonous. My friend answered, "Do you still believe everything some first-grade kid told you thirty years ago?" I thought for a moment, then relented that I possibly didn't know or understand everything about our world. And once again I realized that limited thinking for any reason is the scourge of this earth.

Let's use banana thinking to consider the possibility that we were meant to eat the core of the apple too. Most horses, at least one three-year-old girl, and an average tennis player would agree with this concept. So perhaps you should try it. Perhaps not. But, what do you think? It's up to you. It probably wouldn't be as rewarding an experience as more effectively peeling a banana from the bottom. But eating an apple core could reaffirm the endless possibilities that exist to appreciate new and different ideas.

Is Your Thinking Based On Fiction or Fact?

How many of us have preconceived notions that were formed early in life which really have no basis

25

in fact? I have many more, and I assume you do too. Take for example, apple seeds. No, they are not poisonous. Not only that, but I later discovered some people even eat apple cores on a regular basis to add roughage to their diet.

Is it foolishness that we cling to absurd notions that were formed by our unknowing adolescent minds? Or is it just that we forgot to keep asking questions? We verify many other things in life, so why not verify that apple seeds are not poisonous? Why? Because it takes effort, and because we have to put on our thinking caps to search for the truth. It is much easier to go on accepting an old wives' tale or a half-truth than it is to exercise our minds.

I have a few more confessions to make. The first I will refer to as my ATM story. Automatic teller machines (ATMS) were in widespread use for at least five years before I decided to look into this more effective way to access my bank funds. I initially convinced myself that the machine might be too difficult to operate. But I later discovered that it was really my sheer unwillingness to try something new that kept me from using ATMS sooner.

I was very perturbed at myself when I finally attained my first ATM card. Why? Because after less than five minutes of self-instruction, I knew almost everything there was to know about using this wonderful machine. Even a gorilla could have learned to use the thing. And I had waited five years before trying this more effective way to access my accounts!

A large part of my apprehension had to do with the fact that I was a little slow to jump on the personal computer bandwagon. And I equated learning how to use an ATM with learning how to use a computer. But it is a hundred times easier to use an ATM. Still, I wonder how many people there are who to this very day are apprehensive about learning how to use an ATM for the same reasons I just described.

When I was in college, I was on the leading edge of what is now "ancient" computer technology. But when I graduated and went to work, I began to use the computer a little less each year as I progressed upward into different managerial positions. When I eventually awoke from my stupor, the computer revolution of the past fifteen years had passed me by, and I was considerably less effective than many of my peers.

I used to write everything down on paper first. Even though I knew it would be much more effective to learn how to word process, somehow I never got around to it. It was my same unwillingness to learn something new. But this time there was an added dimension – I knew it would take quite a while to become computer literate, and I am ashamed to say, I was a little bit lazy. To me, it was much easier to go on being only partially effective and use what I already knew, a paper and a pencil. I now call this "conventional laziness."

> *Conventional laziness is a disease that is widespread throughout the world....*

But that is all behind me now. I finally decided to dedicate myself to learn how to word process and use a host of other computer software. So I set myself a

27

goal of one year to become banana computer literate. I attended six computer classes, purchased my own home personal computer, and tried to incorporate my office PC into every facet of my work.

By far the greatest benefit has been the new freedom in writing that I have acquired through using a word processor. I can now write directly from the keyboard to the computer screen, use the thesaurus, move a paragraph at the mere flick of a finger, check for spelling errors, and perform a hundred more tasks with the stroke of a few buttons. Recently I even added an intelligent grammar checking program. Yes – they exist – and they work fabulously.

The result was no more cut and paste. No more rewriting for legibility so my typist could read my scrawl. I became the typist of my own words, and a more effective arrangement I cannot imagine, that is with the exception of voice-to-screen input. I am now an effective word processor because I dedicated myself to learn something new! I wanted to be more effective, so I was willing to pay the price of time and humility to a good teacher. This is the way of the banana.

> *Where did we get such a preposterous notion that we should quit studying and learning after we graduate from our highest level of school?*

Conventional laziness is a disease that is widespread throughout the world. It is mostly attributable to middle-aged people who have for various reasons decided to stop learning and trying new ideas. Take a hard look at yourself. Are there any signs of conventional laziness in your life? If so, then it is time to wake up to a whole new world.

Where did we get such a preposterous notion that we should quit studying and learning after we graduate from our highest level of school? How many people do you know over thirty years of age who have recently learned how to play the piano? How about studying auto mechanics, karate, foreign languages, or ballet at the age of forty? There may be certain physical limitations to consider, but they are not insurmountable. I plan to keep learning as long as I can see, read, talk, and write – how about you?

We need to keep thinking and studying for as long as we live. These activities are very important to our stability and progress. So here are a few more examples of banana thinking that will hopefully convince you that creative thought and an all-out quest for knowledge is the answer to a better future.

The Great Banana Thinkers
Copernicus, Kepler and Galileo

Some superior examples of banana thinking are the philosophers of the Post-Renaissance era who were remarkable for the out-of-the-box nature of their questions.[2] Men such as Copernicus, Kepler, and Galileo were the forerunners of banana thought. Their lives spanned the 1500s and 1600s during a period when conventional wisdom believed the earth was the center of the universe. But these men sought answers to questions that were to result in a break with conventional thinking and eventually redefine the universe as we know it today.

The conventional thinking of that time believed if you were to move in space from the earth to the planets, you would be moving from imperfection to perfection, because the planets were observed to reside in the heavens. All planets were thought to be perfectly round and smooth, and of course at this time in history, there were only five known to man. Each planet was also thought to follow an orbit around the earth in a perfect solid geometrical shape that would fit into a perfect sphere. Great models were constructed to prove this fallacious theory. And it wasn't until Kepler stumbled upon the idea of elliptical orbits that man was to take one of his first steps to better understanding the universe.

Kepler didn't possess a brilliant intellect, he merely worked diligently to determine the answers to a number of cosmic questions. Many of his notions were those of a seeming crackpot, but the few new accurate observations that he spawned more than made up for his failures.

Misconceptions concerning our galaxy abounded during the Post-Renaissance era, many of which had been unchallenged for two thousand years. If you believe it is hard to think anew today, just try to fathom what it was like to change two millennia of ingrained thinking. But each of the aforementioned astronomer/philosophers confronted the very basis of the conventional wisdom of that time. And they did it at the risk of being excommunicated by the Church and ridiculed by fellow scientists. It was heresy to even discuss the possibility that the sun could be the center of the universe. Copernicus found this out when his books were blacklisted by the Church because of his claims that the earth was not the nucleus of the heavens.

These marvelous banana thinkers thought on and progressed, little by little. Their progress was not so much in the realm of genius as it was in the persistence of men in search for the truth.

Kepler's work was later utilized by Sir Isaac Newton to formulate the basic laws of physics that we know today. The earth has rarely been blessed by such genius as Newton. He is one of the few habitual banana thinkers in our history books. Yes, many others have come up with a few new ideas, but it is an exceptional man or woman like Newton who can do so consistently. One could make a good case that there has been no real progress in pure physics since Newton's discoveries, that is with the exception of Einstein's theory of relativity.

True Banana Thinking

We need to ask ourselves if there are more physical laws to discover. True banana thinking would have to say there are certainly unexplained phenomenon that crop up every so often. And true banana thinking would have to ask, "Could it be possible that we don't know it all? Could it be possible there is so much more to learn that the immenseness of it would be hard for us to comprehend?" The answer to these questions is an unequivocal banana yes.

Man has made the same mistake throughout his existence by assuming he has discovered absolute answers to the universe. But we have really only scratched the surface on the book of knowledge. The only thing that can stunt our growth is our own unconscious prejudice and a lack of imagination.

For example, there is a battle being waged today between banana thinkers who are proponents of cold fusion and conventional thinking which favors hot fusion. Fusion energy is one of the great technological hopes of mankind because the fuel (hydrogen molecules) is found in common sea water. It is the next logical progression after nuclear fission. It could mean a cheap, clean, environmentally sound, abundant (as our oceans) source of electrical power.

It takes close to one hundred million degrees Fahrenheit to start a conventional fusion reaction. So you can probably imagine how difficult it would be to contain such heat. The reaction has to be contained in a magnetic field where it exists only in a plasma state. It is easy to visualize the technological problems involved with sustaining such a reaction, let alone harnessing it to produce power.

Cold fusion is a molecular interaction that has been proclaimed to heat water at room temperature in a controlled laboratory environment. The potential of this concept is staggering. Imagine for a moment a small cold fusion generating device the size of a standard outdoor air-conditioning unit that could provide electrical power for your entire house. Or how about a smaller unit the size of a spare tire that could power an electric automobile? This is innovation! But many scholars of conventional wisdom say it is impossible. Nevertheless, the concept has been formed, and some success has been declared on a small scale.

One of the primary problems with developing cold fusion is measuring the output of the small laboratory reactions. Such measuring devices are still fairly primitive, and at the present time scientists are merely measuring a temperature rise, not what creates it. We have to find new ways to measure if we are to invent better machines. I surmise that the fusion equation will remain unsolved until banana thinking scientists decide to concentrate on perfecting fundamental low-level radiation measuring devices first, and cold fusion second.

It may take another hundred years to develop conventional mega-hot fusion into a usable energy source, but cold fusion could power our automobiles and homes five to ten years from now. All it would take is a break with tradition to think the concept through. Of course, one of the problems with this argument is that we still don't know if the idea is true.

Time will tell, but will it be sooner or later? Hopefully the next generation of innovative thinkers will see beyond conventional wisdom and master the measuring device that could not be perfected today. When this happens, cold fusion will be just a few ideas away from perfection, and we will most certainly be on our way to a new and different world fueled by an endless supply of cheap energy. This could be a world of fantastic man-made habitats with a multitude of continuously operating gadgets and cities suspended in mid-air made possible by an infinite power supply. Would this be a better world? We can only hope. But in the final analysis, whether it is proven or not, the concept of cold fusion is a timely example of banana thinking.

It really doesn't matter whether an idea proves to be sound, or an absolute failure. It is the forming of the idea that truly matters. We may fail a thousand times before we come up with that next original proven idea, but we have to keep trying. It is this cycle of trial and error that provides one of the few processes by which we can improve the chance of success and our level of awareness. We must continually exercise our minds through creative thinking if we are to succeed as individuals, as organizations, and as a society.

Banana Thinking Challenges Conventional Thinking

The majority of us are in search of new ideas. We long for improvement, and we understand that our full potential can't be achieved without such progress. But we can only realize our full capabilities through changing our view of the world and challenging conventional thinking. We can achieve our goals and experience this enrichment through true banana thinking.

34

So go forward with your ideas. Think of new ways to enjoy your existence. Find your true place in the world, then sow the seeds of knowledge and help your fellow man build a magnificent tomorrow.

It is time to take charge of your difficult world. You have to take responsibility for your own level of awareness and education. You have to make it happen. Learning new subjects and ideas is the best way to forge a better life for yourself. And your public library or nearest book store is a good place to start. Most likely you will find everything you need at either of these think-tank outlets to dispel worthless superstitions and acquire the wisdom that will help you become a true banana thinker.

CHAPTER 3

Blue Blood

I remember the time at the ripe old age of ten years when I tried to convince my thirty-year-old brother and his wife that my blood was blue. It was something a friend in grade school told me. It seemed logical enough, because even to this day when I look at the veins in my arms, the substance that flows in them appears to be blue. What my grade school friend told me was that blood was really blue until exposed to air, at which time it turns red.

So there I was trying to convince my well-educated brother of something preposterous, until he finally made the point that I was not only wrong, I was ridiculously wrong. Then he explained how he had once seen a blood transfusion in which clear plastic tubes were used, and that even though the blood hadn't yet contacted the air, it was red. That was good enough for me, so I quickly replaced my grade school fable with a plausible fact. I did this for two reasons. First, because a knowledgeable person had presented me with witnessed facts. And second, because I trusted my brother's knowledge and

> *The blue blood incident made me realize at a very young age that I shouldn't believe everything people tell me.*

37

experience more than my friend's, who had fabricated the story anyway.

The blue blood incident made me realize at a very young age that I shouldn't believe everything people tell me. I also realized that from then on when I heard something, I should think it through before adopting it into my personal storehouse of knowledge.

I decided some twenty-eight years later to write about this idea to explain how it affected my view of assimilating new beliefs and information. And when I did, a nursing student read my blue blood incident account and challenged me over something she had read about blue blood in a biology textbook. One of her principal arguments was that drowning victims often turn blue due to the lack of oxygen in their systems.

So once again, I was thrown into a quandary. I thought I had resolved this issue decades earlier, but someone was now slapping me in the face with an old alternative view. Had anyone else made this argument, I would have likely discounted the story. But this woman was a nursing student whose knowledge and reasoning I greatly respected. Still, I was compelled to ask myself, "Was there really blue blood, or was this other person misinformed?"

So I decided to talk to a friend of mine, who is a medical doctor, in an effort to resolve the issue once and for all. I selected an M.D. because of the vast anatomical education that must be undertaken to assume such a title. My question was simple, "Is there ever a time in the human body when blood is the color blue?" He told me there is no time when the color of blood is blue. I was also instructed that veinous blood, which has not been oxygenated, is a burgundy color, and that arterial blood is bright red due to the effect of oxygen within it.

Next I asked, "What causes the body of a person who holds his breath for an extended period of time to turn the color blue?" I was told that the blood becomes evacuated of oxygen and assumes a deep burgundy color and that this combined with pigmentation effects of the skin renders a blue color. Once again I was elated to know that the blue blood fabrication had been sufficiently settled in my mind.

I had been confused over this once before in my life, and this time I was determined to put the issue to rest. So now I decided to go to the nearest university library to perform additional research. My efforts produced many references to blue babies, blue whales, blue this and blue that, but nothing on blue blood. I finally confirmed what the doctor told me. Now I was totally satisfied that my blood would never be blue.

The Blue Blood Concept

I call the kind of thinking that must take place to appreciate the preceding story *the blue blood concept*. It can be broken down into the following ideas. There are often misconceptions which are formed about our world that have no basis in fact. Furthermore, we must seek out our own answers to these basic questions about life and be satisfied that our conclusions are accurate. Without such review our knowledge becomes defective, and our conclusions are often based on erroneous hearsay.

> *We need to remember the blue blood concept every time we are presented with a new idea or a differing opinion.*

Of course, my story is also based on hearsay. However, both of my tutors were carefully endorsed because of my knowledge of their previous correctness in other matters. We must learn to be good judges of knowledge givers in order to adopt sound information. I also performed an adequate amount of research to confirm what I had heard from respected sources.

Blue Blood Is Everywhere

We need to remember the blue blood concept every time we are presented with a new idea or a differing opinion. Subjects as complicated as nuclear fusion or as simple as mowing the lawn can fall prey to the concept. If you listen to people utterly and thoroughly, you will discover that blue blood is everywhere. Yet, in reality, it doesn't exist. So you must determine the color of your own blood, then not be too surprised when you learn that it is really some shade of red. When you further scrutinize your life fluid, you will find its other characteristics are what make you an individual with your

own antibody contingent and a host of other defin-
itive genes and chromosomes.

It is likely there are many blue blood concepts
that have unfolded in your life. Have you reviewed
these ideas, or have you simply accepted what other
people say as the truth? Please don't misunderstand
my question. We must all trust that one another
speaks the truth, but accepting a new idea without
considering its authenticity is where many of us go
wrong. It is truly an ambiguous process in which we
must consider all new ideas and adopt many of them
after they are justified through our own reasoning.

We shouldn't plagiarize the conclusions of others. We need to crunch and grind what we hear
through our own minds in an effort to reach our
own truths. We need to perform our own research
through book learning, getting in touch with our
own minds and bodies, and through discussions
with knowledgeable people. Then if we reach the
same conclusions it is all the better because we will
have to some extent – verify the thoughts of others
with our own reality.

Without such a system of checks and balances
we would be stuck in an environment of flat world
– the earth is the center of the universe thinking –
witch burning – aerodynamic doubting – apartheid
supporting – COLD FUSION SCOFFERS. If we are to continue to grow, we must overcome our cult ideologies
and think for ourselves at all costs.

There are areas where the blue blood concept
runs into a brick wall. These are the times when we

must accept on faith alone that what we are told is true. It takes a certain amount of faith in God and mankind to make any sense out of our world. But we must think for ourselves instead of letting others do it for us. If you believe in God, read His book. Don't simply believe what others say about Him. If you want to learn from men, study their views. But faith must be based on what we *understand* about what we believe if it is to be firmly established in our lives. We must not adopt theories, dogmas, or other doctrines concerning how we should think and live without genuine research and honest reflection.

I am not trying to be dogmatic here. I am merely trying to show you a different way of thinking without giving you all of the instructions to go with it. You must incorporate your own ideas into this line of reasoning to form your own conclusions.

And I am certain that sometime in the future my blue blood story will again be challenged. But that doesn't bother me because I now feel that I possess enough knowledge to defend any argument on the subject.

The only "logical" argument I think I could come up with today in defense of other-than-red-colored blood would be that of the pointy-eared Vulcan science officer on the starship *Enterprise*. Spock's blood is green, or at least that's what I've been told....

CHAPTER 4

What You Live For

Now that we are ready to look at things in new more intelligent ways, it is time to take a look at how we live our lives.

Otto lives to eat bananas. But what do you live for? Is it to come up with that next great banana idea? Is it to realize a lifelong goal? Do you live to make and spend money? Do you live for pleasure? Do you live for your family or simply for another? Do you carry a special burden for humanity? Or do you simply live for yourself?

The true banana thinker should feel free to ask these questions, and not be afraid to hear the answers. If it is truth that we seek, then we first must deal with the basic truths of our own existence. Only after obtaining satisfactory answers to these questions can we live up to our true potential.

Some would say, "We should never live for the sake of another man, woman or child." Others would say, "We should live for one another." Our individual philosophy of life truly matters. There are as many ways to live a life as there are people on this planet. But because we often expect others to live up to our standards, we have severely limited our options in this area. So we have to allow people to create their own environment and live their lives on their own terms according to their own capabilities. If we are compassionate about our lifestyle and are convicted of our ways, maybe we will win a convert. But even if we don't, we must allow others to choose their own way.

Having More Fun in Life

Shouldn't we be having more fun with our lives, children, friends, and family? Life has become extremely complicated in the last fifty years. People of the early 1900s and preceding eras had the primary concern of survival, and there are still many today who are waging this battle. However, many people have been fortunate enough to overcome this problem.

Take the average American family for example. We have ample food, clothing, shelter, two cars, and an afghan hound. So what do we have to worry about? What is our greatest problem besides the health of our physical bodies?

The answer is boredom. We are bored with our existence. Most of us have no life-threatening problems to deal with, and the few that we have are mostly due to our own choosing. Many of us have begun to ignore our fellow man and turn to unproductive sources of amusement. Some of us turn to drugs, others to adrenaline highs, and still others of us withdraw into our own little microcosm where we feel safe, yet are barely functioning.

We long for meaning in our lives and we are searching for answers. Yet we have barely formed the questions. The first question then should be, "Why am I here?" Most of us seek to answer this question, but we fail because we are hoping the answer will magically teach us how to live the rest of our lives.

I would wager that if we took a world poll, the majority of people would simply answer, "I am here to be happy; that's all I want out of life." What a meager want – but one that is so hard to attain. And to many, life is as simple as that. Of course, life is not that simple. But if we choose to ignore happiness in our lifestyle, we can fall off into the deep end of existence and enjoy our life so little that we may as well be dead.

> *The first question should be, "Why am I here?"*

Happiness is a very important part of life – the happiness of family, friends, and people we don't even know. Fun, enjoyment, play, these are the fulfilling things about life. And it is in those times when it is hard to see the fun in an activity that we have to remember our happiness philosophy the most. When times get rough we have to remind ourselves that any endeavor can be made into a sort of game if we try hard enough to make it fun. Life can be the most serious game in the world, or we can live it with a smile on our face and a fun-loving attitude.

The basic point to be made here is that people can get too serious about their existence. Sure, life is a struggle at times. But no one said it was supposed to be easy. We don't want it to get too easy anyway. We can get very lazy when we are given what it takes to survive. We need just enough strife to make life interesting. It gives us the initiative to figure out how to make it fun.

The Happiness Factor

There are many people living in big cities who are happiest when they are experiencing nature. So why do they live in these concrete catastrophes? Wouldn't they be much happier living and working with nature on a daily basis as farmers, forest rangers, or gardeners? If you live in the country, but think you would be more happy striving in the city, go ahead and try it. But don't forget the serenity of a mountain stream, the beauty of a patch of wildflowers, or the sounds of a quiet country evening.

Why do unhappy people go on accepting a less-than-fulfilling existence? The answer to this question lies in the notion of taking ownership of one's present state of affairs. Once we realize that we chose the path that led to an unhappy situation, we become considerably more powerful with respect to changing the situation. After all, if we got ourselves there, it only stands to reason that we can figure out a way to make ourselves happy in the present situation — or completely change it for the better.

There is another problem brewing in our modern world. People aren't happy with their jobs. They aren't happy with their pay. They aren't happy with their families, and they certainly aren't happy with themselves. Most likely the job is the real culprit. How can anyone spend eight to ten hours a day, year in and year out, in a job he or she really doesn't love?

Nevertheless, many of us do that very thing. We must break free from such damaging behavior to ourselves, our families, and our society to search for jobs that fit the way we work and think. True banana thinking can enable us to seek and prepare for jobs that allow us to live the way our heart tells us we should live.

> *People need to be employed in a job they like, in a profession they love.*

People need to be employed in a job they like, in a profession they love. Surely the average person's on-the-job performance and enjoyment of life would soar if such a thing were true. So we need to put people back to work in jobs where they have a passion for performing superior work.

The concept of pay for performance should also be involved in this discussion. In Chapter 9 we will look at the broader issues surrounding pay for performance, but for now let's take a look at the progress of our society.

The Progress of Society

A fellow runner and I recently got into a discussion concerning different categories of philosophy. At the end of our conversation, he asked me a very profound question, "Why has our society made so little progress in the last two hundred years, while our technological achievements have been so staggering?" I had no quick answer for such a question. An inquiry like this deserved some thought.

So I pondered this philosophical matter for several days before attempting to answer his question later that week. I told him I believed our social progress has been slow because there is no reward system for living as an individual. Either we conform to society's rules, or we are thrown out. Certainly there are self-rewards, but society as a whole doesn't condone pure, unadulterated thinking. Either it has to make money, or it has to solve the grandest of problems then put dinner on the table. But there is no "pay for thought," as I call it.

Take Henry David Thoreau for example. He lived meagerly. He prided himself on building a house and living for the best part of a year on $25.22, which was a feat even in his time.[1] I would like to see him try such a plan in one of today's cities. He would most certainly end up living in a cardboard box and eating food scraps from the garbage can behind some restaurant.

> *...society as a whole doesn't condone pure, unadulterated thinking.*

Maybe Thoreau could still survive today if he lived in the country. Things haven't changed that much on a Walden Pond that is waiting to be discovered in Kansas or Ohio. He could probably still borrow some of the neighbor's tools, find a quiet forest for lumber, and build his own furniture.

Possibly this shows us that the country is where we should be living today. People have always needed wide-open spaces so they can breathe freely and walk fifty feet in any direction without bumping into anyone else. We do need the company of other people. But if you put one million people in a twenty-square-mile area, the quality of life for the majority of them is bound to falter.

Maybe this also shows us that what was possible yesterday all over the world is still possible today, and that we just have to look harder to find our oasis. Peace is waiting for those who are willing to explore and discover.

I had a related experience during a recent trip to a well-known movie studio in Florida. The studio had hired several unknown actors to work as zany street people to make conversation and joke with guests who were touring the grounds. When I encountered one of them while buying an ice cream bar for my son from a street vendor, he slapped a nickel down on top of the ice cream freezer, then asked the ice cream lady in a nerdy voice, "What can I get for this?"

Never being one to pass up a good straight line, I replied, "The only thing that will buy you is what's on the lady's mind." So he quickly asked the lady what was on her mind. He did it four times in a row, but each time there was no reply.

Then his attention turned quickly to me as he pummeled me with the question. So I finally answered with the most outlandish double-talk I could produce. "What's on my mind," I responded, "is, why, with such a quantum leap in technology,

49

have we experienced so few strides in social progress!?"

His answer was swift and surprisingly appropriate, "I suppose it is because we have focused more on material things than on people." I knew truth when I heard it, and my ears had just been blessed with something basic, but very true.

In fact, this is exactly what we have done. In our present society we have replaced men with labor-saving machines. We have built taller skyscrapers and bigger and faster airplanes, and we have devised a thousand ways to extract precious minerals from our earth. But we have made few and feeble attempts at optimizing the quality of individual performers.

We push harder to teach more to our young people at an earlier age, and we value knowledge. But we still don't value thinkers. We push our children toward conformance when we should be encouraging them to be creative. I am not deliberating about which color of playdough our children should be using. I am merely suggesting that we throw away their modeling clay and encourage them to dig up a plate of mud or bowl of sand every now and then to work with in forming their masterpieces. Then and only then can they create their own sculptures by looking at things from the bottom – and the top – of the banana.

Maybe it's just an illusion. Perhaps we have made similar progress in both technology and social behavior. Perhaps there is only a perceived advance in technology compared to that of human effectiveness. But if this is the case, there must be quantum leaps yet to be made in the technological arena. And if this is true, there will be a great need for as many banana thinkers in the future as possible.

Find Yourself

You must form your own questions after reading this chapter, then search for the answers. You must explore the wisdom of the ages to attain your own piece of mind, then try to fit what you find into the human equation of interacting with other people. Humanity is the focus – your own – and that of others. People and all other living things are what is important in this world. A life is priceless, and yours should not be wasted because of a lack of understanding, pessimism, or an abdication of enjoyment.

So first you must find yourself. Then you must endeavor to enjoy life at a very basic level. Get too complicated, and you will lose the meaning. Ask too few questions, and you will be ineffective. But if you can achieve a balance between being, learning, and doing, you have a good chance of finding happiness.

The True Meaning of Life

The true meaning of life is found in the heart. It is found in being and loving in a manner that truly makes you happy. There is not just one way to be happy. We must endeavor to live and love as our hearts tell us or our happiness will be flawed. We must think as our wandering minds would have us ponder, instead of conforming to the structure of others.

Who is happier, an unfulfilled man or woman who earns a good salary, or a person who lives in the mountains, has no job, and lives day by day enjoying nature and all that it has to offer? Who is happier, a garbage collector who loves his work, or a corporate executive who works half-heartedly and never looks for a better situation because what he or she has is a safe way to earn a living?

True banana thinking will sift through the blockages to true happiness, then explore and take the appropriate action to find and be yourself. But there are so few who actually have the courage to do it. What are we afraid of? Is it failure or what others will think of us? Neither of these excuses hold water.

If you are afraid of failure, then think about this. If you persist in following a course which is not of the heart, you may find mediocre happiness and some wealth of the spirit in the short term. But when you are old, you will look back on your dreams and remember what your heart told you to do, and sorrow will fill your soul. You will realize that a lifetime spent with an unfulfilled heart was a failure — a failure in the ultimate sense because time can't be reversed. You have to set yourself on the right course now before it's too late and you have no more heart left to give or time left to give it.

There is more to this life than brick and mortar. There is more to living than flesh and whim. If your heart yearns for something, don't deny the kind of banana thinking that will help you seek it out. Find a job where you can express yourself and contribute from the heart. Don't settle for mediocrity. Seek your true place in the world. Follow your heart and be happy. This is the way of the banana.

CHAPTER 5

Banana Thoughtfulness

Otto is a thoughtful gorilla. He picks up after himself, he takes care of his brothers and sisters, and he really and truly cares about every member of his family. Perhaps it is not that difficult to be thoughtful when your feelings are confined only to the fourteen members of your family.

Human beings would probably be a lot more thoughtful if we were just one big family. But isn't that exactly what we are? No matter whose account we subscribe to, we all originated from the same place. We have common roots and are of the same family. So simply treating each other as such would solve many of today's social problems.

One of the most important things you and I can do to increase the level of caring in our world is to show other people that we care. When one person cares for another, it often causes a chain reaction. The person cared for demonstrates caring for someone else, and that person in turn cares for another, and there we have it, a chain reaction of good will.

> *Do a good deed every day.*

I have always liked the slogan, "Do a good deed every day." The phrase embodies the idea of people

55

caring for other people. Just think of the caring chain reaction that would take place if everyone performed just one good deed on the same day. Perhaps that happened recently, and the result was the fall of the Berlin Wall. Maybe there was a measure of infinite caring that took place when the Soviet Union disbanded.

Helping Other People Is the Banana Way

You can only be effective in caring for other people if your disposition is good. Therefore, you need to stay motivated and always think positively. Try to look at problems as opportunities to be good to others and always endeavor to treat other people as you would treat a member of your immediate family.

Helping other people can be personally rewarding too. The brightened perspectives of people you have helped will make you more effective because they will be more willing to help you achieve common goals. Therefore, in simply being good to other people, you will be increasing your effectiveness, while at the same time gaining the satisfaction that another person is better off because of your supportive attitude.

We Look, We Think, We Be

We look for truth,
And settle for halves;
We covet youth,
And eternal laughs.

 56

We look to the sky for answers,
But we have not posed the questions;
We are runners, doers, and prancers,
And things we cannot mention.

We are everything,
And we are not;
We want it all to be,
But we forgot,
The best parts of life are helping others,
Because they are all our sisters and brothers.

Putting Banana Thoughtfulness to Work

There are abundant opportunities to help other people. The following are twenty-four brief suggestions of how you can put banana thoughtfulness to work for the benefit of all:

1. Don't just do favors for favors. Be selfless. The highest level of caring is when you do something for someone that is unexpected, without expecting anything in return. Be a giving person. Take advantage of all holiday gift-giving opportunities, and look for other occasions to give gifts. Enjoy giving presents more than receiving them.

Have fun, but allow others to have fun too. Care more about their enjoyment than yours. Do you have to get your way all of the time? Give in once in a while.

Revel in the time that you helped another rather than the time you were helped. The beginning of every day is a new opportunity to be good to someone.

Don't judge others, help them. Write them, call them, visit them, listen to them. Other people could be the most important part of your life.

So you've given them your money, your blood, your old clothes, and your time. What's next? Give them your heart. Be good to people, and people will be good to you. "And in the end the love you take is equal to the love you make."[1]

2. Tell people often that you care. Everyone needs to be reassured and reinforced. Your loved ones need to hear it, and you need to say it. Display your love, your goodwill, and your delight toward others.

What if a good friend or family member were to die tomorrow? Wouldn't you want that person to know how you feel today? Tell him or her now so that you will have no regrets for good tidings left unsaid.

3. Remember most people want to be liked and are basically good. They should not be ignored or thought to be insignificant. So enjoy others to the fullest. They are necessary for your survival and enjoyment. What an unimpressive world it would be without other people. If you were the only one living on planet earth, who would you aspire to be, and what purpose would it serve for you to achieve your life's goals?

 58

Who you are is directly related to the people in your life. Your family, friends, neighbors, and working associates are all part of you, and you are part of them. You touch so many lives without even realizing it.

Take for example the movie, *It's a Wonderful Life*, starring Jimmy Stewart in which he portrays George Bailey. A guardian angel grants (for a short period of time) George's bitter, self-pitying wish that he had never been born. When he does, George discovers the enormous number of people who are adversely affected because he never existed. Put yourself in George Bailey's shoes and think about a world without you. Would it be better or worse? Hopefully your influence on the people around you would be missed.

Think about your spouse who you never would have married, and the love that never would have been shown to your children because they never would have been conceived. Think about how your parents never would have been able to share your joy. And consider how your workplace would have been without your influence and how your neighborhood would have been without your goodwill.

What condition would the world be in today without your presence here? Hopefully the world is a much better place because you are here and helping others. This too, is the way of the banana.

4. Accept individual differences. What a boring place it would be if everyone were the same. Realize that people are inherently different, so endeavor to

understand them. Try looking at situations from their point of view.

Picture in your mind a world in which everyone lives the way you do. They all have the same job, take the same route to work every day, wear similar clothes, drive the same type and color of car, and live in the exact same kind of house. How boring and how unimaginative that would be.

5. So maximize your opportunities. What have you done for someone lately? Did you do something memorable? Think big. Give people something that's so much a part of you the thoughtful occasion will live on in his or her mind.

6. Perform at least one good deed every day. Be good to a stranger.

7. Do charity work. Give of your money and *yourself*. Of course you must support yourself and family first. But once you have achieved a reasonable level of sustenance, find an outlet with which to assist others.

Just a few hours a week of your time could mean the difference between the happiness or sorrow of a needy senior citizen, a physically limited child, a mentally handicapped person, or a family in need. You must find a way to help other human beings who are less fortunate than you. Through banana humanitarianism you will move a step closer to understanding the true meaning of life.

8. Be good to all children. Forgive them constantly. Validate them. Be good to your own children as well as to those of others. They are our future.

 60

You can help shape the caring adults of the future by being good to children today. So help them grow. Tell your children you love them. Show your affection for them often. Look for opportunities to make a big deal out of a small success, then hug and kiss them and tell them they are good.

9. Don't get mad, be glad. Be consistently good-natured. If you are consistently kind to other people, they will want to be around you. This will perpetuate itself because the more people there are in your proximity, the more opportunities you will have to be good to others.

10. Turn the other cheek to those who would torment you. Show them you are strong by confronting pessimism with optimism.

11. Be courteous and say you are sorry, if it is warranted.

12. Be courageous. Even though you are supposed to be tough, you can still show others you care.

13. Always be honest. Tell the truth. Have integrity. Do what you say you are going to do. Be trustworthy. Keep your word. Be punctual. Meet your time contracts.

14. Get out of that rut. Surprise your spouse. Take him on vacation or fix her an impromptu dinner.

15. Be helpful. A friend in need is a friend who should be helped. Maybe his or her deeds have helped you when you were in need. Return the favor.

16. Don't say bad things about other people. If you can't say anything good about anyone, then don't say anything at all. If you have a matter of conflict with someone, deal with that individual directly to resolve it.

17. Say hello and good-bye.

18. Listen to others. How can you help them unless you know the facts?

19. Feed people. Buy them dinner. Give them food. One route to people's hearts is through their stomachs.

20. Smile *a lot*.

21. Take time to explain. Tell other people why you do what you do. Do this not so much to seek their approval, but because you want them to understand you. Endeavor to communicate. If you didn't get what you wanted, then ask why.

22. Pick up the mess. You may not have made it, but wouldn't you like the environment to look better? Pitch in and help clean up that unsightly clutter. This kind of banana thoughtfulness works with general litter, your children's rooms, your neighbor's yard, or any mess that needs cleaning up.

23. Slow down and lighten up. It seems as though people are always in a rush to get where they are going. I am continually amazed at how little compassion is shown by other automobile drivers. Most people won't give an inch. It's like there is some unwritten rule that they have to get where they are going before the next guy. What does it matter if you

arrive at work or at home a few minutes later, when it means you have taken the opportunity to be good to another person?

I think we would enjoy our drives more if we would let other vehicles crowd in front of us every once in a while. Decide to enjoy your travel time. You will be forever traveling through life, and if you don't take time to enjoy every moment, you may miss a large part of what you are intended to see.

> *Slow down and lighten up.*

24. Look for positive statements in your environment. I recently saw a billboard that read, "EVERYTHING HAS ITS BEAUTY, BUT NOT EVERYONE SEES IT." I wonder how many people really took the time to read that sign? How about a bumper sticker that reads, "HAVE YOU HUGGED YOUR CREW TODAY?"

That reminds me of a license plate I recently saw while driving down the interstate. It read, "ALL KIN." My immediate thought was that it meant that we are all related with respect to the story of Adam and Eve. Then I thought about it a little more, and the meaning expanded considerably.

"ALL KIN" can mean many things, and they are all good. It means we should make love and not war, because we are ALL KIN. It means we should be good to other people, because we are ALL KIN. It means we should treat others like family in our personal and business dealings, because we are really ALL KIN. It means we should do a good deed every day to help another, because we are ALL KIN.

"ALL KIN" are two powerful words that world negotiators could well remember. It is truth in every sense of the word. We are all brothers and sisters. We are the family of this planet. Everything we do to our earth affects our fellow inhabitants. In almost every breath we take there are molecules of air that have been in another's lungs. We are close. We are here to help each other.

Be banana thoughtful to those around you. If you haven't been so inclined in the past, start with a smile. Then start being sensitive to serve people's needs. They will love you for it, and you'll feel better too.

CHAPTER 6

Mind, Body, and Unity

Otto knows that his survival depends on a sound body, keen instincts, and a knowledge of his environment. He has no permanent shelter, no material possessions, and no medicine. His very existence depends on his flesh and all of the gray matter he can muster as he finds himself attempting to live in harmony with – yet concurrently opposed to – the full force of nature. One broken arm or a forgotten direction could mean his demise. So he must rely exclusively on his mind and body, and on the help of other gorillas, to buttress the dangers of the wilds.

The Most Basic Maintenance

The majority of us have a roof over our heads when we need it, labor-saving devices to assist our toil, and medicine if we require it to heal our bodies. There are books to read, documentaries to watch, and schools to attend in an effort to expand our minds. Yet, many of us refuse to support the most essential parts of our mental and physical being. Our minds and bodies must be maintained if we are to live long, happy, and fulfilling lives.

We should devote equal amounts of energy to each of these areas of our existence if we are to maximize our effectiveness. But many of us put one before the other. Some do it chronically. Brilliant scientists are often overweight, and the most muscular among us are often mentally deficient. Therefore, because it is hard to believe that anyone really wants to be obese or illiterate, we must consider why people neglect these most basic components of existence. And we must ask ourselves, "What compels us to fail to implement the rudimentary steps that could increase our personal effectiveness, thereby enabling us to make ourselves and our families happier?"

Could it be that we are so busy living our lives through and for other people that we don't have time for self-maintenance and improvement? If this is the case, banana thinking must cause us to pause and consider the possibility of living first for ourselves, in order to do what is truly best for others. There is a proper order in the way of the banana.

This may sound a little selfish, but if you honestly consider the alternative, it is likely that you will understand the difference between primarily focusing on your effectiveness, or fragmenting yourself into certain mediocrity.

If you don't devote attention to these essential parts of your existence, namely your mental and physical faculties, sooner or later you may find yourself unable to provide for your family. And you may be considerably less capable of experiencing life in

 66

the manner you desire. But if you choose to concentrate on attaining your physical and mental potential, you will most certainly be approaching maximum effectiveness with respect to providing for your family and the other people you care about.

Check Your Priorities

You need to make sure that you get your short and long-term priorities in order. In the short-term realm, if your son or daughter were to break his or her arm, you would certainly be justified in living for your child for a period of time necessary to get through the trauma. If your immediate family needed you to participate in a family-oriented event in lieu of your participation in a personal exercise session, then of course the proper response would be to please your family.

But it is not these sort of infrequent interruptions to your schedule that are the issue. It is the routine instances that arise daily and interfere with your personal maintenance and development regime that you need to regulate. You have to plan and schedule time for yourself in the form of body and mind maintenance, or suffer the consequences of a mediocre **you** trudging through an unfulfilling life.

Taking Personal Responsibility

Wouldn't we be better off if we recognized early in life that we make ourselves what we are? With this realization would come the understanding that if we want to change what we are, we must put forth the effort to make it happen. It's not an easy task, and I am not entirely convinced that happiness would be any less complicated to deal with if it were free from strife and sacrifice. I am convinced, however, that if we don't decide to create our own future, others may create it for us.

Taking personal responsibility is the issue. You have to be willing to do whatever it takes to change yourself for the better. You can reverse the trend of self-pity and low self-esteem, but you have to do it for yourself. There is no one who can to do it for you. Neither your mother or father can do it for you. Nor can your children, your friends, or your work associates. Not even God will transform you into the shining physical specimen with superior intellect you could choose to be. You have to take control of your physique, your mental capacity, and your life. Only you.

> *Wouldn't we be better off if we recognized early in life that we make ourselves what we are?*

The Value of Exercise

Today's world teeters with out-of-shape workers. They are out of shape mentally as well as physically. With the average worker putting in fifty to sixty hours per week including commuting time, there is little energy left for leisure reading – and even less for exercise.

 68

Even if you do possess the time and energy, there are other demands on your time such as children, personal finances, your spouse or close friends, and the upkeep of your dwelling and automobiles. There is little time left to get that workout you need, or to finish that book you started two months ago. So what do you do?

First of all, you have to plan your exercise periods in advance: then let nothing stand in your way of implementing your plan! With regular exercise you have an edge, but without it, you are average at best.

Vigorous exercise is one of those contradictory things. Those who understand it will tell you that when you exercise on a regular basis, your energy level will be higher than when you are sedentary. They will also tell you that the more energy you exert in the form of exercise, the more energy you will have at your disposal to exert. You may feel drained for a short period after exercising, but if you exercise regularly, your overall energy level will be much higher than that of an inactive individual. It is somewhat like the sought-after perpetual motion machine where more energy comes out than goes in. An inspiring level of energy can be built and maintained through frequent exercise.

Regular vigorous exercise also helps control weight, allows for sounder, more refreshing sleep, and leads to the reduction of stress. Sometimes it even produces a sense of euphoria (runner's high). In addition, it aids the digestive cycle, improves

69

muscle tone, and provides important cardiovascular benefits.

Banana Running

Probably the best exercise on a minute/benefit scale is running. Thirty minutes of running four times a week, plus a few supplementary weight and isometric exercises, is all that is needed to keep trim and fit. Some people who live to run would swear it is their fountain of youth.

When you run, you are proving to yourself that you can go the distance – in life, in sports, and in thought. Running is the ultimate synergy of mind and body because only through mental fortitude can you push your body to the limit.

The nonrunner is often fooled concerning the boundaries of his physical capabilities. But the runner knows his boundaries because he approaches them often. The habitual runner becomes addicted to these periodic releases of energy and anxiety. He lives to feel his body rhythmically striding in the great outdoors, or running on an indoor track where fellow exercisers can see the splendor of human locomotion.

When you run, you are proving to yourself that you can go the distance — in life, in sports, and in thought.

Running is a wondrous activity in which mind, muscle, and fortitude push the body to the limit of its capabilities. Your body was built to run, so use it and enjoy it.

 70

Finding the Time

A common problem of the person who is considering the addition of an exercise routine to his or her busy schedule is finding the time to do it. Granted, it is difficult to find time to exercise, but if you really want to do it, you can do it. The time is out there, you simply have to find it. It's probably hiding in your lunch-hour and in some poorly spent time over the weekend.

So first of all, try lunch time. Find an exercise club (with a shower facility) close to your work and bring a meager sack lunch on exercise days. Schedule three days during the work week and exercise once on the weekend. Take that hour on Saturdays that you are sort of watching television and reading the paper at the same time while contemplating what to do later, and there you have it. Not only will you be burning calories during one of your regular hours Monday through Saturday, you will also be consuming less food afterwards. So you will be getting your exercise as well as implementing a diet of sorts.

If you can't fit exercise into your lunch routine, then you must find time before work in the mornings, or right after work before supper time. If you choose to exercise after work, here are a few options:

Find an exercise facility that is located on the route home from work and use it two or three times a week. You could also rush home, put on your jogging gear, and put in a few miles before supper.

71

If you do have to wait until later in the day to get your workout, there are several advantages to consider. The first advantage comes from running on an empty stomach, which is what you should always do. In so doing, your heart has only your active body to service without a stomach full of food to digest. The second advantage is because you will be running before you eat supper, your appetite should be slightly curbed, so you will eat less. The third advantage of exercising before supper is that you will be less likely to postpone it until tomorrow due to fatigue, which is brought on by the regular activities of the day.

But wherever you find it, you *must* find the time to exercise. For people who exercise on a regular basis, there is always time to swim a few laps, put in a few miles, or play a set of tennis. You may get to the point where you are addicted to something that is good for a change. You will crave your every-other-day run, and you will find a way to fit it into your changing schedule. It will be high on your list of priorities. It will be so because of the benefits you have proven exercise time to produce.

Eating to Live, Not Living to Eat

You may eventually get to the point where eating is put lower on your list of priorities than regular exercise. When this happens, you will know you have arrived at the right balance of exercise and the other aspects of your life.

 72

The majority of us don't get enough exercise. But we all overeat from time to time. Many of us do so daily. Eating is instinctive because it is necessary for our survival. So when you can learn to put it on hold, you will have truly taken control of your physical destiny.

Life is full of learning experiences, and there are some that must be repeated over and over again. Overeating is one of these experiences. About every month or so, and more often for some of us, we overeat. After we do so, we remember for several days, or even weeks, the bloated, wretched feeling that accompanied our overindulgence. Eventually the memory of our overeating fades until we forget what it was like to have gorged ourselves to the point of agony and displeasure. Then we overeat again, and the cycle repeats itself.

The Twenty Minute Rule

The majority of overeating is caused by what I call a faulty full sensor. Our full switches activate about ten minutes too late. Let's say the average meal lasts thirty minutes. If we would realize we should eat for only twenty minutes because that last ten minutes of eating is where we go too far, there would be much less overeating in the world. But we continue gorging ourselves for the full thirty minutes and come away from the dinner table in need of an antacid.

If you are trying to control your weight, think about this twenty minute rule the next time you sit down to a full-blown meal. Try to cut off that last ten minutes of eating, and you will walk away from the table fortified, but not overfed. Don't trust your *full* sensor, because it will fool you every time you think it is telling you it is okay to keep eating.

Banana Thinking "Breakfast"

Now let's discuss breakfast for a moment. Many have tried to convince you and me and the rest of the world that we have to eat breakfast to remain healthy. But I challenge you to reevaluate this notion. I do believe there is some credence to the growing-kid theory. But for many adults breakfast provides non-essential calories, and many have found they can maintain or lose weight much easier if they don't eat it.

I came to this conclusion based on my own personal experience. I found that I can function very well in the morning without eating breakfast, but that if I falter and begin to eat it consistently again, my mind and body begin to crave it. I prefer to maintain a body weight that is very close to what my physician recommends for my height and frame. And for me, the problem with eating breakfast along with two other meals a day, is that I gain weight. Therefore, I have concluded that breakfast food is better left in the cupboard in my house.

But as I have stated, you have to determine for yourself what works and doesn't work for you. So what will it be in the future – breakfast or no breakfast? You make the choice.

 74

The point of this discussion is to put eating lower on your current list of priorities. You need to fuel the human furnace to provide adequate energy to maintain your performance. But when eating becomes the most important thing in your life, you have failed at proper banana thinking. You have failed because in seeking to fulfill yourself through food, you are building an enormous body that will soon overload your heart, feet, and lungs. It may also keep you from the banana actions that could help you succeed.

Eating should not be an urgent issue. So don't feel compelled to eat at regular intervals. Don't be one of those people who get cranky when they don't get to eat every four hours. Eat only when you feel the need, and I am not talking about every half hour or so. Eat to live, don't live to eat. And when you do, eat a balanced diet to maintain energy and vitality.

Banana Reading

When you get to the point that your energy level has peaked because you are exercising on a regular basis and you have gained control of your weight through better eating habits, the way of the banana would say that it is time to devote part of your extracurricular activities to reading. I would think something on the order of three books on different types of philosophy, three full-length novels, two self-help books and two technical journals per year, along with various magazine articles and short stories would be sufficient to feed the mind of the average four-year college graduate.

If you have achieved higher levels of education, then sustenance for your mind will take more effort. If you aren't a college graduate, then concentrate your reading on one theme at a time until you feel comfortable with a subject, then move on. If you already read more than I have suggested here, you can expect to expand your mind on an exponential scale. But if you read less, or not at all, your base of knowledge will erode, and you will fall behind in a world where there are infinite possibilities for those who are willing to study.

Banana Learning

There are also a variety of other ways to learn besides reading. Reading should be the primary focus, because books and other reading materials are the most widely available source of knowledge. But you can also learn much from experimentation as well as through auditory and visual knowledge sources. Television documentaries are an excellent way to expand your mind.

So be the kind of banana thinking person who makes things happen. There are too many people in the world who expect success to come to them. You must work toward it. If you wait for it to come to you without any effort on your part, the days, months, and years will pass you by as successful people leave you behind.

Growth is all-important in our lives. First our bodies grow, then our minds need to grow. It takes a lifetime to fill a mind. If you are not constantly trying to fill yours, then you are missing one of the essential elements of a fulfilling life.

There are different languages to learn and histories to review. There are a multitude of biological creatures to study and millions of people to understand. There are millions of books to be read and even more to write. There are philosophies to question and ideas to be unfolded. The possibilities for growth are endless. All you have to do is set your course, then see where the prevailing winds will take you.

The Way of the Banana May Send You Back to School!

If you wish you were in a certain profession, then determine what it takes to qualify yourself for that type of career. Go back to school if you need additional education. Obtaining additional education is the most significant thing that anyone can do to change the direction of his or her life, yet many people avoid making the commitment. They side-step putting forth the extra effort that could get them where they really want to go.

Some people are afraid of school. They are afraid of failure, and they are afraid they might not be smart enough to learn. All you need to know is that you can learn anything if have the desire to achieve and the discipline to apply yourself. It may take

77

incredible persistence, and it may be slow going at first, but you can do it. Banana thinking will prevail.

Banana Writing

Reading, studying, and schooling are essential to build a base of knowledge, but there will come a time when you have read and analyzed enough. It will be as though your mind is overflowing, and you will have to spit out some of the information you have gathered back on the world before you absorb more. Reading is good, but writing can be very fulfilling. So write. The more you write, the better you become. You may even want to take a few writing classes on the side.

When you write about your thoughts, experiences, and desires, they take on new meaning. Putting things down in black and white forces you to solidify your ideas and to contemplate your position on specific issues. Writing is personal therapy for the mind, body, and soul. And writing is one of the few ways that you can truly create. You can devise whole new worlds through the written word. You can win on paper what you have lost in reality. You can establish the principles on which to base your life. You can escape into fantasy worlds, or visit ancestors in times before you were born. You can establish new personal philosophies, then tear them apart through the world's greatest critic – yourself. You can even give a shot at foretelling the future.

All of this is within your grasp of the nearest pen or computer keyboard. You and you alone can be the creator. The power wielded by the mere flick of your fingers can be unmeasurable. With the stroke of a pen or keyboard you could be the architect of a completely new universe and your imagination could feed the minds of many.

Banana Sleep

This chapter has been about the importance of exercising the mind and the body. As we conclude it, another point that should be brought into the discussion is our need for adequate sleep. We will talk about this in greater detail in a following chapter entitled "Stress Liberation." So for now let's leave it at that. But don't overlook the importance of your nightly sojourn into Never Never Land. If you regularly get less than seven to eight hours nightly, you are doing your body a disservice. One way to ensure your full banana effectiveness is to get sufficient sleep.

The Choice Is Yours!

Now that we have discussed several ways to become more effective, you are faced with a choice. It is you who could choose to ignore what you have just read, and it is you who could choose to implement certain needed changes that could make you considerably more resourceful. You can choose to plan a new exercise program, then go to the nearest library to pick up a few good books. This is the way of the banana.

79

Please don't choose to remain on a course that is ineffectual and possibly self-destructive. So what are you waiting for? The world has never stood still for you. You have to keep turning with it. You know what you have to do to improve yourself, so don't put it off any longer. Begin building a better banana today!

"If there is any common ground here, it has to be as demonstrated by our gorilla friends via the golden rule."

CHAPTER 7

Gorilla Ethics and the Golden Rule

Gorillas, like other mammals and animals that live in family units, possess an uncanny sense of ethics. Ethics geared to their small gorilla world, but ethics nevertheless. Their standards include sharing with, caring for, and protecting other family members through something very similar to what we call, The Golden Rule.

Gorillas are very cognizant of treating other gorillas as they would like to be treated.[1] I have observed similar behavior in zoo and barnyard animals. So, once again we should take a lesson from our fellow inhabitants of this earth.

There is so much beauty in our world. There are deep blue oceans with so much to give, and there are forests rich and green, teeming with life. Our mountains rise high creating wonderfully clean habitats, and our soil grows food in so many varieties that eating is a delight. We value our own existence above all others, and we should. But we must also understand, help, and love our fellow earth inhabitants.

Let's discuss the concept of human beings having dominion over animals, mammals, and all other living things on the earth. I presume we have been granted this right because we are the only living creatures on the planet that are supposed to possess a sense of our own existence. But what about whales, dolphins, dogs, cats, and elephants – just to name a few? How did they get left off of the self-awareness list? I am certain that many other living creatures on this earth are capable of thinking, learning, and self-appreciation. Therefore, because Otto thinks; he is entitled to live.

How arrogant we have been to slaughter the other living things on this planet as we have plundered at will, and devastated whole species.

Morality, ethics and arrogance don't mix.

Animals, mammals, and all creatures that roam upon or fly about the earth have a right to live. We as human beings have no right to play with the existence of other living things. Morality, ethics, and arrogance don't mix. A large part of the ethics matter is the understanding that all living things which exist on our planet have rights of existence just as we do.

We generally accept the vile treatment of non-human living things on this earth without any thought. Such thinking closely parallels our previous discussion concerning Copernicus and many of his cohorts who were severely ridiculed for claiming that the earth was not the center of the universe. We

 84

look on such events with an incredulous sneer that anybody could be so stupid, and we go on thinking our own barbaric thoughts without any attempt to challenge our contemporary beliefs.

We have to improve the manner in which we view supportable facts and superstitions if we are to improve the manner in which we think out of the box. We have to do so because unless we are able to judge for ourselves the differences between the two, superstition will continue to win. It will continue to thrive because we are unwilling to look past the box, which is what we must do before our minds can travel beyond it.

In biblical teachings God has granted man the right of dominion. I do not wish to refute this right or to go against the will of God. However, the concept of truth is often ambiguous. Who can say what God really wants, but God? I love my God, and I sincerely want to do and think as He wishes. However, man has severely muddied the waters. There is much written that is from man, and some, I am told, that is written by other men that is truly inspired by God. The only problem is that sometimes it is difficult to tell the difference.

So whose ethics are we discussing? Is it the ethics of other men, or the ethics of the individual? I believe in the latter. Deep inside every one of us beats a heart that is compassionate and empathetic to other living things. We must link with our own hearts and try to understand our individual ethics. If there is any common ground here, it has to be that

85

which is demonstrated by our gorilla friends via the golden rule.

Men and Women Working Together

Another issue in today's world is that of men and women working together. I can't help but believe that we have recently lost some of our effectiveness with respect to such relationships. It is almost as though men and women are afraid to enter into casual discussions nowadays because they are fearful of being misunderstood. And we are spawning an atmosphere of non-communication between genders in our workplaces.

To achieve anything close to peak effectiveness, we must encourage all people to communicate freely in their jobs, at home, and in public places. Freedom of speech is one of the basic rights that our forefathers recognized as having been bestowed by God on all people no matter what their circumstances. Much has been sacrificed for this precious right.

We need to practice free speech because it is effective that we do so. People have different opinions, preferences, and ideas. It is through being exposed to a variety of them that we can form more complete opinions and ideas of our own.

I agree that blatant sexual advances and unwanted physical contact are improper behavior. But I think we have gone too far. We have eroded the possibility of the wonderful nonsexual relationships that can exist between men and women. When done honestly and appropriately, a casual relationship between a man and a woman simply makes the job a little more enjoyable. It is fun to understand and recognize the differences between men and women. Our differences are readily apparent and must not be ignored or belittled.

The reason men open doors for ladies is not because they think members of the female gender are too weak to do so for themselves. Men open doors for ladies because they merely want to be polite to another person, and opening a door is a customary way

> *Men open doors for ladies because they merely want to be polite...*

to do so. Likewise, women don't casually jest with men for any other reason than it is a pleasant way to carry on a conversation.

Gentlemen need to be gentlemen, and ladies need to be ladies, and we can do so in an environment where people can speak freely and honestly without the fear of a lawsuit. We need to capitalize on the strengths of each gender to be more effective in our working relationships rather than foolishly creating adversarial situations. This too, is the way of the banana.

Unity

The founding fathers of these United States had a vision in which people from all walks of life could come together as a nation to help one another flourish. For two hundred years Americans have lived that dream. We have positively influenced the rest of mankind, and now the world has become a much smaller place.

So think about how you treat your brothers, sisters, parents, or children and use that same posture in dealing with all other people. You wouldn't cheat your brother, so why cheat any other man? You wouldn't insult your mother, so why insult any other woman? Simply be good to other people and treat them as you would treat a relative, or better yet, treat other people as you would have them treat you.

Trust

We should endeavor to trust our fellow man. Trust is an essential part of ethics. If we honestly believe in the goodness of men and women, then we can trust them. But if we are pessimistic concerning this aspect of humanity, we will likely trust no one.

To be an effective individual, you have to trust the people around you. If you are a manager, you have to trust your work associates. If you are an individual contributor, you have to trust your supervisor. If you are married, you have to trust your wife. And if you are a parent, you have to trust your children.

We become terribly ineffective when we don't trust others. We become ineffective because we have to check and double check to see if another's performance is meeting our expectations. What is the worst that could happen in most situations? The answer is that someone could fail to perform as desired. Someone could make a mistake. Oh no! Not that! But whoever said it was a perfect world?

People are supposed to fail. That is how they learn. We have to let them do so, and we have to trust them to do it right the next time, in the right way.

Integrity

Integrity is another important component of ethics. If people are to trust us in the future, we are going to have to follow through with what we say we will do today. This is very difficult for some people. Time commitments are the most frequent commitments we make, and often the hardest to meet.

Take for example a person who frequently tells someone he will arrive at a certain time, and he is habitually late. Someone else may tell a working companion that a certain project will be finished by a certain time, and the project is not only late, but it is never started. Don't these people understand the detrimental effect this type of behavior has on trust?

The bottom line is you have to do what you say you are going to do on a continuous basis if people are going to trust you. I have heard that a righteous man will ponder before he answers others' questions. With this knowledge we should take the time to think through our schedules and other commitments before making any new ones. Then once we have, we must honor our word. If you can manage to perform in such a way for a significant period, the trust that people will bestow upon you will be staggering. And you will be more effective because of your integrity.

Airplane Encounters

I like to meet people, and if I have an occasion to discuss ethics with a new acquaintance, then all the better. I thoroughly enjoy what I call airplane companionship because it is inevitable that a few such meetings will take place when several hundred people are crammed into such a small space. I have had some of the most in-depth discussions concerning philosophy and other subjects with people on airplanes. There is something about that type of environment which makes people want to bare their souls. Maybe it is the risk of flying that causes people to feel that there is a slight chance it may be their last conversation. Or maybe it is the notion that they will never see the person next to them again, so it's all right to tell him or her their innermost secrets.

Price Versus Principle

I was traveling on an airplane several years ago and was fortunate enough to be seated by a drug enforcement officer from Florida. Somehow the subject of ethics came up. So I thought I would bravely ask this person whom I had just met if he had a price. His answer was immediate, and his answer was, "yes." He qualified it by saying that his personal price included enough money to buy his own island, which he estimated to be at least $100 million. But the problem was, he had not yet experienced a situation in which that kind of money was involved. He said he got close once, but that he told the drug dealer there wasn't enough money to make him stray

 90

from the law, and he suggested that the drug dealer would probably have to kill him to get him out of his way. Our conversation then quickly turned to another subject. But I assumed because the officer wasn't living on his own island, and because he was still alive, that the situation must have rectified itself and his ethics were still intact.

Are You For Sale?

The point of this story is that every person has a price. The price may not involve money. It can range from attainment of love or material things to the realization of a lifelong goal. Most of us say we are ethical because our prices are too high and we rarely get into a situation that tests our integrity. The few people like that drug enforcement officer who frequently get into those types of situations have thought it through, and they know their price. But others, who are rarely exposed to such potentially life-changing ethical decisions, may set their price too low if a situation arises.

You may be confronted with such a situation some day. So search your soul now to determine your price. If you fail to think it through beforehand, you could end up paying for it dearly, even with your life.

Don't misunderstand the meaning of price versus principle. We must all possess a set of principles by which we exist as moral human beings. These principles are very important and should not be set aside easily. There comes a time in all of our lives where we have decisions to make with respect to our principles. And there are overriding concerns that arise from time to time, when we have to decide whether to go with the moment – or to follow our principles.

There are times when it is necessary to sacrifice the moment for your principles, and believe me, there are also times when the moment is so true that a principle may fall to what your mind or heart is telling you to do. These are some of the most difficult situations in life. The point of this discussion is that you need to be firmly planted in what you believe and even act out a few such situations in your mind before the real-life situations come to pass. They come your way nearly every day in business. So if you have gone through a couple of dry runs, you will be prepared to deal more effectively and honestly with difficult ethical situations when they actually arise.

The problem is, to many, the difference between right and wrong is rarely absolute. A better deal very often overshadows good business ethics, and one's personal ethics in dealing with others are frequently put to the test. Therefore, it is up to each individual to make his own determination and live by his own code. The true guide in dealing with all aspects of ethics is as follows: "Do to others as you would have them do to you."

PART II

Banana Concepts
at Work

CHAPTER 8

Risky Business

Otto the gorilla was spending another day in the trees. Often he would raise his head to the sky and let out a mighty roar as if to challenge all of nature that he was indeed the master of his own destiny. He thoroughly enjoyed the exhilaration of swinging from limb to limb. Once in a while he would even miss and fall onto his bountiful posterior. But whenever this happened, he would immediately climb back into the trees and resume his performance, without recognizing that he had ever been on the ground.

Otto knows that he must risk failure to enjoy his life. And he knows instinctively that he must risk himself often to increase his odds of survival in his savage banana world. His behavior coupled with a natural sense of boldness produces an uncommon willingness in Otto to take risks.

Another great lesson to be learned from our remarkable friend here is the importance of risking failure. But maybe we need a more precise and identifiable example. Maybe Jack Quest can help us grasp the full meaning of the concept.

*"What we have to do is put our ideas at risk
whenever we have a chance."*

 96

"Risky Business"[1]

Jack Quest is his name and taking risks is his game. Jack, a super secret operative of the Queen's Super Secret Service, was investigating for the British government on the case of the "Missing Egyptian Idol." Jack had traced the priceless object to the city of Bokonon, Hungary, had confronted the thieves, and had subsequently recovered the priceless artifact.

And now he was returning to civilization in a small twin-engine aircraft. He was taking a nap. But Jack was suddenly awakened when someone grabbed the front of his shirt and pulled him from his seat. Yikes! He quickly realized that he was being thrown from the airplane – without a parachute, and that his assailant had also jumped from the plane – with the idol and wearing a parachute.

The air screamed by Jack's ears as he plummeted through the stratosphere. As he free-fell he knew there was only one desperate possibility for escaping his fate. So he gathered all of his courage, put his arms at his sides and flew toward his would-be murderer. His killer, unaware that Jack had gained so much airspace on him, was greatly surprised when someone grabbed for his parachute. So he kicked him away with a swift movement of his leg.

Jack tumbled through the air at least five times before he righted himself. But as soon as he regained his balance, he aimed himself and flew toward his adversary again. And again Jack was thwarted by the thief, but this time he ended up just above him. Jack wasn't about to give up because the alternative to his attempts was a certain, flattening death. So he regained his composure, then flipped himself around in mid-air smashing his boot down hard on the nose of his opponent, knocking him unconscious.

Jack then retrieved the parachute, strapped it on his back, and with only a second to spare before pulling the rip cord, he reached out to grab the idol that was miraculously suspended between the two during the scuffle. Jack's parachute opened about the time his assailant awoke to find himself helplessly falling to his death. This was just another risky adventure for Jack Quest. He was used to risking his life for glamour, queen, and country. What a guy.

Ten Years Later

Jack Quest is his name and taking risks is his game. Jack is now working for a large corporation in the United States. He is to attend a meeting in which many fellow employees and several managers are to discuss differing ideas concerning how to cut costs and increase corporate revenues.

Jack has a few ideas he thinks would be of use to the company. So when the opportunity arises during the meeting, he speaks up with an idea that only *he* thinks is well founded. And because the concept is completely off the wall, he receives a sneer from almost everyone in the room.

But Jack has confidence that his ideas are sound. So he contributes another idea, and then another, until he hears someone say, "Hey, that's a good idea," and then someone else adds, "What if we did that plus attached an energy-saving device too?" Jack's idea turns the meeting into one of the most productive idea-generating sessions the company has ever seen.

Jack is certainly happy he didn't let one failure stop him from putting forth the rest of his ideas. He learned long ago that persistence is an important part of effectiveness, and that if you fail, you have to keep trying again and again until you succeed. This was just another risky situation in which Jack Quest risked his ideas and his pride for the good of himself and the company.

Today at Your Company

Just like Jack Quest, we work in a risky environment – one that has never been more difficult or challenging. Many companies have lost momentum and are having trouble regaining it. Others are still trying to apply outdated concepts that worked twenty years ago, but barely meet the demands of today's quicker paced and constantly changing business world.

Maybe they just got tired of expending the effort it takes to succeed. Or maybe they have simply forgotten what it takes to be a winner. The solutions to such problems require today's employees to be innovative and to come up with a multitude of new ideas and different approaches.

99

Perhaps your company is ahead of many of its competitors at this time, but what will the future hold? Will you continue to lead the pack with respect to expenses and infrastructure? Or, will you slip into a sea of mediocrity?

One way to ensure success is to learn the lesson of Jack Quest. We must learn to more effectively risk ourselves and our ideas. But risking our lives in the course of our job duties is not the issue. What I am referring to are those frequent opportunities we all have to risk failure.

Not every idea we conceive is a Nobel-prize-winning notion. Some ideas are bound to fail. In fact, a person who is not failing on a regular basis is probably not living up to his true potential. We severely limit ourselves when we are afraid to think new ideas. We sit trapped in a mediocre cycle of stale concepts that have lost their luster and have nothing more to offer.

> *Every time we fail, we are afforded a new opportunity to learn something about the nature of what we were attempting to do.*

But every time we fail, we are afforded a new opportunity to learn something about the nature of what we were attempting to do. With this new-found knowledge we can conceive better ideas based on new data to possibly come up with that one-in-a-thousand concept which can flourish into a very successful achievement.

100

Using this line of reasoning, we can relish our failures because they may lead us to great success.

For many people, risking failure is analogous with risking their job and livelihood. To fail is bad. Therefore, anything that could result in a failure is avoided. People who think like this never grow and rarely experience success on any measurable scale. They are afraid to stretch themselves and to test their ideas.

At least part of the answer to improving the overall effectiveness of your organization is to convince your employees to adopt a sound risk-taking attitude. I am not talking about gambling your company's assets or putting anything at risk other than your own pride. Pride is the most undesirable of all attributes. It frequently discourages us from taking calculated risks because we are afraid to be wrong, which would most certainly bruise our delicate egos.

Mediocrity and Pride: Strange Bedfellows

It is that same pride, or "fear," for lack of a better description, that keeps us from speaking up during a meeting when we have a better idea. It is the fear of telling our bosses that we perceive their ideas to be wrong because we might be at risk of reprisal. Pride keeps us performing projects that nobody really wants to undertake because we are afraid to risk our ideas against someone we perceive to be an authority figure.

101

Mediocrity can take hold in the risk-fearing environment. Therefore, flexibility should be one of our primary concerns. We need an environment where people have the courage to tell their supervisors what they think – especially if their supervisors are wrong. And this does happen occasionally, because nobody is immune from making a mistake or a poor decision.

Mediocrity can take hold in the risk-fearing environment.

The best thing that can exist in a working relationship is the kind of candid attitude that allows each person to tell the other if he is wrong. We have to reverse the sort of non-confrontational attitude that causes us to allow a person to walk around with a "kick me" sign on his back without anybody telling him. This is the reason a person won't try to improve the way he works because he is afraid someone will think he is stupid if he fails.

We have to overcome our fear of failure. Many small failures are essential to gaining knowledge and understanding which ultimately provide us with the means to succeed. So we should put our ideas at risk whenever we have a chance. We have to encourage timid idea generators to speak up, and we must realize that the price for our own silence could be more than we can afford to pay. Only by risking failure can we flourish and survive the next quantum leap in business effectiveness.

An Additional Risk-taking Concept

There are many types of perceived risks in our world. Men and women torment themselves greatly over that which doesn't exist. Some people visualize a catastrophe is about to happen when in fact there is no risk at all. Others could sleep through a tornado without any thought of danger.

The majority of the time a perceived risk turns out to be the combination of a reluctance to take risks, and a lack of knowledge. We must overcome the use of perceived risks as a crutch that fosters indecisiveness or supports an unwillingness to take reasonable chances.

We must also learn to recognize when our knowledge is the limiting factor in a situation. It is always better to base risk-taking decisions on personal knowledge. But there are also many instances when we have to trust the opinions of others, use our best judgment, then take the reasonable risk. Much more on the concept of risk taking is contained in Chapter 15, "Intuitive Risk Taking."

CHAPTER 9

The Compensation Game

"RIAR! RIAR! RIAR!"

Okay, enough animal sounds. Let's get down to business. "The Compensation Game" is next. What you see is what you get, and what you get is what you earn and what you ask for.

"The Compensation Game"[1]

A person can't work for the primary benefit of another person. People have to be paid at a level commensurate with their job responsibilities, and individual contributors must be rewarded for their performance. But this is not the case in many of today's companies. The result is a semi-productive workplace where mediocrity is common because there is little reward for extra effort.

Money is not the root of all evil. It gives us something to strive for and is a means to compare our general success in the world to that of others. The reason people strive to obtain money is the same reason they strive for freedom. Money and freedom are analogous in that sense. If you have enough money, you are free to go where you like and do what you like on your own timetable. Individuals who do whatever is necessary to get paid for their performance will ultimately have greater freedom of choice.

Is there a place for performers in the business world of the 1990s?

The middle class of American life is slowly decaying. A new wealthy class was created in the 1980s with a doubling of the number of millionaires and a tenfold increase in the number of billionaires.[2] And as the difference between the upper and lower classes becomes more pronounced, the problem of individual contributors obtaining their fair share becomes more alarming.

It is as though we are working on a life-sized game board called "Work Hard You Fools!" where the rich get richer and the poor get poorer. *They* are consuming your work, and *they* are inadequately rewarding you for it. Who are *they*? *They* are the people who are keeping part of your paycheck. *They* are your federal government officials who have borrowed the country into a recession and have severely mismanaged your country's wealth. *They* are the people living in opulence who tell you that you must work for less because your company can't afford to pay you what you are worth.

So what are you going to do about them? Can you convince them to pay you what you are worth? Is there a place for performers in the business world of the 1990s?

106

There are bilkers too. Bilkers are those people whose level of contribution to a company is hard to discern. They are everywhere, and their earnings are comparable to yours. Bilkers come to work every day in an unproductive stupor, then when they go home after every payday, they take home compensation that should rightfully be yours because you work much harder. The only way for employers to eradicate the bilkers is to make a real effort to determine who they are, then weed them out. That's right. Employers need to have enough backbone to fire people who are not fulfilling their job duties.

The problem is that many times upper managers or owners of businesses are oblivious to those who are taking them for a ride. It is the grassroots workers and performers who know the identity of the bilkers, because they have to put up with their incompetence every workday. Therefore, a strong grassroots movement is necessary in any effort to rid a company of non-performers.

We are living in a society that sometimes parallels the *Atlas Shrugged* culture created by Ayn Rand in the 1950s.[3] Ayn Rand envisioned a culture where non-performers took and took from the performers until the performers pulled out of society, and the business world collapsed. I would never advocate any such pulling out of society. However, the similarities between what happened in *Atlas Shrugged* and what is happening today are startling.

But who is going to speak up because the performers in today's society are not being rewarded for their efforts? Who is going to say, "I'm mad as can be, and I'm not going to take it anymore?" It should be you and me, and everyone else who is poorly compensated for individual performance.

Maybe the question should be asked, "Is there anybody who really cares?" Have we possibly become so numb to the issue that our hopes to be fairly compensated have all but faded away?

There should be a realm where thinkers thrive, performers achieve, and innovators create. It can be achieved if all performers stand up for what is right and refuse to take less for our work than what we know it is worth. True banana thinking shouldn't come cheap.

Various women have spoken up over the last thirty years concerning fair pay for their jobs, but little action has been taken. In 1986 women earned only $.64 for every dollar that men earned in the United States.[4] And this trend is likely to continue until business women *everywhere* become animate and outspoken concerning their dilemma. High-achieving women want equity just like other performers.

> *There should be a realm where thinkers thrive, performers achieve, and innovators create.*

Men and women quit their jobs for the same reasons, to get ahead.[5] They feel they are falling behind because they are not adequately rewarded for their performance. So employers must realize the substantial contributions of performers to their companies.

And they must consider the negative effect on earnings that could occur with the attrition of true performers from their staffs.

In many of today's companies it is a common situation for employees to be paid with respect to seniority instead of performance. It is likely that many such situations exist in your workplace. Is it fair to pay older employees more than their younger counterparts for the same type of work? This is something we need to banana think about. It is a similar kind of question to the one posed concerning equal pay for men and women in the work place.

Should We Reward the Old for Doing Work at the Level of the Unskilled Young?

The continuing saga of the racial compensation gap[6] should also be considered. Why is it so hard for the executives and business owners in charge of today's payrolls to understand that people want to be paid fairly with respect to their performance? Young or old, male or female, black or white, people with similar experience should be paid comparably for the same job if their performance is the same. And the performers that contribute more to a company should be paid significantly more than people who are not so productive.

Why do you think people in business for themselves work so hard? It is because they reap the total benefit of their labor. If they work eighty hours a week instead of forty, the impact of their extra effort reflects on their earnings. But this is not the

case if you work for someone else. In the sub-
servient work environment it is very difficult to be
compensated for extra effort – and this breeds mediocrity, my friend. It spawns mediocrity because no
matter how hard you work, your compensation is
linked to a system that is designed to support the
unproductive bilkers – not the performers.

Where bonus incentive programs do exist, they
are frequently ill conceived[7] and there is little quan-
tifiable connection between the job that was done
and the bonus compensation that was received.[8]
Therefore, bonus incentive programs of the future
should be individualized and structured much looser
than the precision plans of today. As a banana
thinker, I envision a new era in which you will rate
your own performance, write your own additional
compensation request, present it to your supervisor,
then expect him or her to act on your situation. In
this sort of work environment, if you don't get the
additional compensation you think you deserved, or

**Speak up
and be
heard.**

at least a reasonable explanation, you
would have the right to take your case
to subsequent levels of management.
You could take it all the way to the CEO
or to the owner of the company if necessary.

Speak up and be heard. Don't take less than is
fair for your work or services. You have to be true
to yourself, and only you know if you have been
fairly compensated. It is no longer taboo to ask for a
raise if you think you deserve one. The *comparison*

monster is a ruse, fabricated to keep you from comparing your level of compensation to that of others – so you will be satisfied with less. To heck with the comparison monster. Make those comparisons. How are you going to keep score unless you compare yourself to others? Make your dissatisfaction with your level of compensation known to your employer if you feel you are inadequately paid compared to your peers.

Salaries are kept secret in most companies because there is disparity in the pay of employees in similar positions. But I think everyone's salary and/or bonuses should be posted for all to see. This would inspire many questions concerning differing levels of compensation between individuals performing the same type of work. Then the differences in pay could be openly discussed and explained – even readjusted!

It is not just a matter of being purely motivated by money. People are motivated in many other ways. But when it becomes difficult for people to meet their basic obligations and needs, this is when the desire for money becomes inherent. And this is what is happening to many performers today. The non-performers are taking too much from what should rightfully be going to the performers, so they are forced to speak out on the subject of performance pay. But are they? Are you?

More often than not, good things come to those who ask. But those who fail to be heard will most certainly be left behind in the compensation game.

The concepts that you have just read are important to all performers and are very important banana concepts. They apply to school teachers and social workers, as well as to stock brokers and technical professionals.

True banana thinking challenges the very basis of our society's fickle compensation system. There are few incentives to perform in any job, much less in the jobs that really matter in our present society. People who choose a vocation in social work or school teaching understand from the beginning that the pay will be small and the hours long. They choose their life mainly based upon the satisfaction of helping other people. I praise these devoted individuals for their unselfish attitude, because it takes workers like these to keep our present-day society from disintegrating.

But banana thinking must ask, "Is it fair that stock brokers earn five times more money than the average school teacher? Is it equitable that the average social worker's annual earnings are only a fraction of that of the average lawyer?" I think not because school teachers and social workers are certainly putting back more into our society than the financial and legal manipulators. And I banana think there can most certainly be fair equity for these occupations if people will simply speak up! But you and I must know when to say when. I know this sounds like so much double-talk. There is simply a difference between most conceptual thinking and the implementation of it.

112

The fact of the matter is, sometimes those who are holding onto the banana's stem just won't let you peel it from the bottom. So you must be able to perceive when it is time to speak, and when it is time to shut up. Politics play a big part in the real world, and if you don't learn how to play them, you will get passed by, tossed out, or put out to pasture.

Some present-day philosophers would say that you should take it "to the max" on all occasions — and if you aren't pushing hard enough to get fired once in a while, then you aren't pushing hard enough. But in our current environment where it is very hard to find a job, I would say it is good enough to push it to a point just short of "getting the boot." This may be a very fine line, and you will be the one to perceive where to draw it.

Stand Up For Your Performance

So stand up for your performance, and by all means be unwavering in your principles. Know when to speak up and when to put it to rest. You can do both if you try hard enough. Just remember that while the squeaky wheel does get the grease, the constantly squeaky wheel gets replaced.

113

CHAPTER 10

The Ultimate Motivator

Otto knows nothing of the human business world. But he really knows much about keeping motivated. He knows that the day he is not enkindled may be the day he is food for the lions. He knows that the law of the jungle is survival of the fittest — survival of the most highly motivated.

A similar climate exists in today's business world. Individuals who fail to remain motivated quickly fall behind the competition. If management falters and motivation is unsupported in the workplace, earnings will surely tumble, and the organization will become easy prey for corporate predators. So finding and supporting the ultimate motivator is necessary for survival.

The Ultimate Motivator

Employee motivation is the key to business success. Executives in many of today's companies are looking for ways to make their employees more effective. They have come to understand that in today's very competitive business world, if you don't continually optimize individual performance, you will fall

115

behind. And if you stay behind for very long, you go out of business. Therefore, management throughout American business has learned that if a company is to succeed, its people have to be motivated.

> *People need a reason to come to work every day above and beyond a salary.*

So how do you motivate people to perform on a long-term basis? Can you provide them with the motivational tools necessary to continually self-activate? Can you create an environment where people want to put forth extra effort? Can you (and should you) allow real freedom in the workplace?

Yes, you should, and...you can.

People need a reason to come to work every day above and beyond a salary. If you want substandard or at most average performance, then provide each of your employees with nothing more than a mundane job and a paycheck. But if you try to determine what motivates each individual and help him achieve his goals, you will make great strides in building an effective work force.

All too often people are only semi-motivated in the performance of their work obligations. They lack adequate self-motivational skills and are refused a work environment where they could choose to perform.

It is of primary importance that people be adequately compensated for their performance. However, supervising people with sensitivity, goodwill, and understanding is just as important as monetary compensation. And building an excellent work environment is of utmost importance to ensuring that motivation is adequately supported.

Therefore, the key elements necessary to inspire people are a high level of self-motivation, and a work climate that girds and perpetuates positive attitudes. People also want freedom. They need to feel that they have control of their future.

Self-Motivation

Effective individuals have to be self-motivating. A worker's ultimate motivation comes from within. No one motivates an individual but himself. It all comes down to a matter of attitude. Others can provide support, but each person must provide the attitude. If he has a self-motivational attitude, then all obstacles can be overcome.

There are very few people who are not to some degree self-motivated. Granted, there are some chronically unhappy people who trudge through life with little to show for their meager efforts, but they still have the motivation to keep on trudging. Successful people are simply self-motivated to a higher degree than low-energy performers.

There is a significant amount of negative energy being generated in the present-day business world because of a lack of job security. In the past, people could count on the same job for life. But today an individual worker is one of the fortunate few if he can remain employed with the same company for ten years.

The majority of today's work force is continually worried about being laid off. People are so worried about their jobs that their minds are not on the business at hand. This often leads to poor performance, on-the-job injuries, and mistakes that result in higher-than-normal operating expenses.

All that anyone can do in today's business environment is put forth his best effort. If he does this and still gets "sacked," then at least he has the consolation of knowing he did his best. There are very few guarantees out there today. But the individual worker will have the best chance of keeping his job and moving up the ladder of success if he keeps performing.

The business world is chronically unfair, but it is geared toward the performer. A performer always has a better chance to be rewarded than a non-performer. And performance is a matter of motivation.

A Positive Attitude

A positive attitude is very important in maintaining a high level of self-motivation. Pessimism breeds failure and mistrust, but optimism generates the opportunity to succeed. That is why it is so important to be an optimist – to look for the good in all things, and to shine in the face of bad attitudes.

Everything has its beauty, but not everyone sees it. What kind of person would you rather have as a work associate – a dismal, complaining pessimist, or a bright and cheery optimist?

118

Could it be that your view of the world is masked by pessimism? If you want the world to be a better place, you must first think good things – then put them into action!

Sometimes you have to look hard for goodness, though it is usually there. But if you have looked real hard, and still can't find it, do something about it. Do whatever is necessary to transform negatives into positives.

Dwell only on good news. If you overhear discouraging information, deal with it in a constructive manner and put it behind you. Don't seek out bad news. That is the way of the pessimist. Bad news procreates pessimism. Don't read negative articles. Don't watch depressing movies. Don't let bad news on TV affect your attitude. They have chosen to report the worst of the worst. So keep that attitude positive, and be an optimist. Your continued self-motivation depends on it.

Self-Rewards

One way to remain self-motivated is to keep your life full of attainable goals and events. Reward yourself by proactively creating something to look forward to. The rewards don't have to be big, and the goals don't have to be long-term.

Self-rewards can take many forms. You can plan a vacation, purchase theater tickets, schedule a shopping trip or a round of golf, make an appointment to get your hair styled, or simply take some time off from work to be with your family. Center your reward around an activity that can be planned in advance. Then you will have something to look forward to. Whether it is slated for later the same day, at the end of the week, or next month, the thought of engaging in your reward activity will help keep you motivated.

...keep your life full of attainable goals and events.

It is likely you have applied the previously mentioned motivational idea in the past without realizing you were actually motivating yourself or someone else. The following is an example of this concept with just a slight twist.

I needed a little motivational boost the other day. I had fifteen minutes remaining on my lunch hour, so I walked into a downtown music store that sold used cassette tapes. I browsed through the inventory for at least ten minutes without really knowing what I was looking for. Then I finally found a cassette tape I had wanted to own for several years. A happy man, I purchased the tape for $3.50, placed it in my shirt pocket, and returned to work.

Back in my office, I pulled the tape from my pocket to show a work associate what a good deal I had made. I remember making the comment that I had no cassette tape player in my office and that I would have to wait until quitting time to play my new tape in the car while driving home. I put the tape back in my shirt pocket.

The rest of the afternoon went great. Every half hour or so I would notice the tape in my pocket and think briefly of how much I was going to enjoy the music on the way home. I distinctly remember performing more work than usual that afternoon because of my heightened level of motivation. And I thoroughly enjoyed my musical interlude at the end of the work day.

I have applied the same concept by looking forward to viewing a video cassette tape of a good movie. Or by calling my wife in the middle of the afternoon to find out what she is preparing for supper, then looking forward the rest of the workday to one of my favorite meals. Or through motivating my six-year-old son with the thought of a fun event to take place later the same day or the next. This concept really works. Why don't you give it a try, or apply it more often?

Self-Challenges and Enhancement

You must keep your expectations high. Never limit yourself or your ability to succeed. One way to get ahead in today's ultra-competitive environment is through self-enhancement. Try going back to school, study how to better take risks, improve your physical conditioning, learn a foreign language, become a proficient public speaker, or participate in some other fulfilling activity.

If your career progress has stalled, you must continue to challenge yourself. One of the highest forms of self-validation is to commit yourself to mastering a new hobby, sport, or other diversion. If you have always wanted to learn to play the piano or pilot an airplane, then start taking lessons now. What better time to improve yourself than when your career progress has decelerated? Fortify yourself with new accomplishments and you will be building your personal arsenal in preparation for the next advancement opportunity to come your way. Those opportunities may be few and far between in the future, but they will come, and you will need to be ready for them.

If you are a highly self-motivated individual, it is likely there has been little time in your life to relax and view matters from a more casual perspective. Your existence has been one achievement after another, and there has never been time to stop to enjoy any of them. So if you can find the time now, rekindle some relationships and reactivate your capacity to learn new things.

...continue to challenge yourself.

Maybe it is time to slow down and enjoy life for awhile until you build up to your next level of accomplishment. Take some time to work on your imaginative skills, learn how to play again, or study the philosophy of being.

If you are one of the many managers who have suddenly been thrown into an individual contributor role, then re-evaluate your direction. Ask yourself, "What is it in business that I seek?" Maybe it is time to strike out on your own. Possibly it is time to change careers. Or maybe you just need to reflect for awhile and learn a new part of your business.

122

Employer Support

Employers in every category of business understand the importance of employee motivation, but they often falter in the development of an environment that is necessary to allow people to flourish. Very often the principal reason motivation is so difficult, is because the management of a company doesn't understand the people they are attempting to motivate. They think they can come up with most of the answers without listening to their people. This is analogous to attempting to learn how to operate a complicated piece of machinery without asking the manufacturer or a previous operator how it works.

So if you want to know how to make the working conditions and environment in your company more amenable – ask your employees. Sure, you will get some outlandish responses. But you will also receive some very good ideas.

You may find that your employees want more modern office equipment, more flexible hours, more company events, a real bonus incentive program, or a more casual business environment or you may discover they simply want someone to tell them they are doing a good job once in a while, or a supervisor who supports innovation instead of hampering imagination.

People truly want to participate in the improvement of their work environment. And they need their supervisors to help them succeed. It is not enough that the company succeeds. The people who make it successful must also benefit and prosper. So the company and the employees must win if the relationship is to endure. A supervisor must show a genuine interest in others. Supervisors should engage employee's minds and help develop their ideas.

If you sincerely want to support your employees, then ask for their input. You would do the same for your customers, so why not do so for your business team? Are they not just as important to the success of your business?

> *All people really want is something to look forward to.*

In the present "downsizing" environment, it is very difficult for people to have something to look forward to. If they don't get laid off, they can look forward to staying in the same job for an extended period because there are fewer positions to aspire to in the company. Still, people have to be motivated to do a good job. To some extent it is a catch-22 situation because they have to be motivated to help create a motivational climate. Therefore, the nineties supervisor must work hard to create and support these changing environments. He has to concentrate on people rather than working most of the time as an individual contributor. The supervisor of today must inspire individual and team performance.

All people really want is something to look forward to. A good people manager defines the aspirations of individual employees, then helps them reach their goals. There is no guesswork here.

124

A supervisor must care as much about what the employee wants as what work needs to be accomplished on the job. Information concerning individual goals is determined through continuing discussions between the two parties. And such dialogue rarely occurs unless initiated by the supervisor. The discussions should be informal, questions should be asked concerning short- and long-term goals, and the employee needs to be given time to reflect on his answers.

Getting motivated can take the form of looking forward to retirement, a year-end bonus, a weekend activity, or simply though a daily work diversion. Take your yearly vacation for example. You plan it, anticipate what it will be like, then when the time finally arrives, you are off in search of relaxation or adventure. Sometimes the vacation is not nearly as good as the anticipation of what you thought would be a great time before you got there.

> *A good people manager defines the aspirations of individual employees and then helps them reach their goals.*

Getting people to set goals for themselves is one of the most important duties of a supervisor. Whether it is attaining proficiency with computer programs, the completion of a team project, or merely some type of personal improvement, a vital responsibility of the people manager should be helping others plan their goals, then supporting their achievement. This should not only include work goals. Personal goals are just as important. If work and personal goals are not in harmony, then both may be in jeopardy.

Charismatic Managers and Cheerleaders

Managers who exhibit a "work-with-me" attitude instead of a "work-for-me" facade are considerably more effective. Such managers are often referred to as, "charismatic," and can do wonders for employee motivation.

Most employees just want to know that they are part of the team. When a supervisor sincerely talks, plays, and has fun with his work associates, he is truly supporting the bond of the business team. Managers should also frequently get out among employees in the workplace to talk about their philosophy and how it relates to the welfare of the company.

(A note to the corporate managers of the world: When was the last time you heard something useful about your organization while sitting behind your secure, wooden desk? Get out of your office and tune in to your company!)

Rah, Rah, Roy — You Can Do It, Boy!

An effective manager must also be an excellent cheerleader. In this context the definition of a cheerleader is a manager who is continually searching for good in every employee's work. A manager who frequently takes the time to address small groups of employees on recent successes or excellent

126

accomplishments. A manager who walks through the office several times a day and tells individuals their contributions to the company really matter. Or a manager who exudes appreciation for a job well done and takes the time to show people that he or she cares about their well-being and performance.

People like to be told that they are working intelligently. So individual and team accomplishments should be pointed out every time a supervisor can fathom a reason to do so. Supervisors should also make the most of every opportunity to tell their work associates that they are resourceful, hard working, have a secure future, and are integral members of the team. This will help support their self-esteem as well as facilitate additional productive behavior.

As a manager you should devote significant energy to helping people in the course of their duties while trying hard to make their jobs enjoyable. On occasion, you may even want to consider chanting like a high school cheerleader. You know, the "rah, rah, rah, two-bits-four-bits, six-bits, a-dollar" stuff. You should do this for two reasons: 1) because you frequently need to add some entertainment to a work activity to make it fun, and 2) because it works.

I remember the time when I went trout fishing with my brother, my brother-in-law, and my nephew near Lake City, Colorado, at Crystal Lake. The fishing was only fair, but my brother-in-law, being a superior fisherman, caught his legal limit in a few hours. He then proceeded to cheerlead to spur the rest of us on to catch more fish. As I recall the cheer went something like, "Rah – rah – rah, fish – fish – fish." And the more he chanted, the harder I fished, then eventually caught my limit too. There was something magic about having what I perceived to be a great fisherman on Crystal Lake cheer me on to success. I found myself not only wanting to catch more fish for my own satisfaction, I also wanted to please my cheerleader as well.

The same concept works for a manager. There is a basic element in all of us that desires approval from family members, friends, and work associates. Managers everywhere are in the people business, and they often have to resort to any means possible to keep motivational levels elevated. So by effectively cheerleading employees, a manager fulfills a large part of his or her job duties.

Motivator Fred

I once knew a man named Motivator Fred,
He could motivate your body,
He could motivate your head.

He was a master of the trade,
As he supervised his crew,
You could count on him,
As everybody knew.

He gave everything he had,
Then he left you alone,

To perform your work,
At your own special tone.

That motivator Fred,
Was a true inspiration,
To all who worked at his location;
He made work fun,
He would say don't look back,
Look toward the sun;
He was a motivating man,
A motivating man –
I liked him.

Personal Freedom

Though much progress has been made over the last two decades, there are many more areas that can be improved to give employees more freedom in the workplace.

For one, the freedom to communicate is still a one-way street in many organizations. Many upper-managers give open-door policies and bottom-to-top communication programs considerable lip service, but they still see these innovations as inconveniences rather than the true way to conduct business.

One sure way to stifle creativity is to ask for ideas, then ignore them.

There are token efforts in many companies to gather improvement ideas from employees. However, solutions to the largest problems are usually within the grasp of management where employee input is either discounted or ignored.

One sure way to stifle creativity is to ask for ideas, then ignore them. So listen, listen, listen to your employees, because they are the true resource of your company.

Most jobs dictate to employees what time to get up in the morning, when to eat lunch, when to return home to their family in the evening, and when to take vacations. They often dictate an employee's attire, his work associates, his hairstyle...and the list goes on and on. Therefore, any restriction that could be released back to the determination of the employee should be considered a restoration of freedom in the workplace.

Why don't you make your own list and restore as many freedoms as you can to your employees? They will feel emancipated, and their productivity will soar.

Additional Suggestions for Employers

If you have a vision for effectiveness, share it with your employees and incorporate their suggestions. Work with your people to determine where to optimize your business. Guide them with your wisdom and show them the way. Then leave them alone to perform as only they know how in their arena of expertise.

People are looking for happiness and meaning in their lives. So if you want to increase their

130

productivity, help them find it. Cater to their happiness and show them why their productivity matters to the welfare of their company.

You also need to be fair, honest, and trusting with your employees. Keep them informed with frequent updates on the status of the company and the current business environment. And when in doubt, apply the Golden Rule. Treat other people as you would have them treat you. If you demonstrate that you are genuinely interested in their well-being, your people will put forth extra effort to please you, and ultimately, they will be motivated to succeed.

The ultimate motivator inside of every individual is just waiting to be focused on greater effectiveness. Each person has control of his or her own motivational destiny. So sustaining a proactive attitude with the purpose of staying motivated is the key to success. And employers can choose to support or hinder this attitude.

One way employers can nourish effective motivational attitudes in their employees is by providing satisfying working conditions. People who are supported in their bid for continued self-motivation will generally be more effective. But those who continue to work in an environment that is confining and non-validating will eventually be battered into mediocrity.

Employer support is vital. Still, motivation is ultimately something each individual must do for himself. The sooner you embrace it, the better off you will be, because *you* are the ultimate motivator.

CHAPTER 11

Who Are the Real Customers?

I t rains, then the sun shines, and the banana trees bear their fruit. The green bananas eventually ripen to the point where they contain all that nature intended, protected by a yellow skin. When Otto picks a banana from the tree, it is as though he has walked through the doors of the nearest grocery store to obtain his favorite food. He is truly the customer of his surroundings.

In a similar sense, all of the animals living in Otto's jungle are customers of one another because it takes each of them to comprise a balanced environment. In striking yet another parallel, the environment of a company, is just like Otto's jungle. In constantly changing roles, the employees of a company have an opportunity at one time or another to work as customers of each other. This can be an important concept that contributes not only to individual effectiveness, but to the effectiveness of an entire organization.

"Who Are the Real Customers?"[1]

Who are a company's real customers? Some people may say the stockholders. Still others may think

133

of the general public who buy the company's products. Both of these groups relate to the literal definitions of outward "customers" in the realm of the retail business world. But banana thinking would push the concept one step further. It would push it inward. So let's banana look at the idea of customers from a different point of view. Let's look at it from a perspective that relates the concept of customer relationships to business organizations themselves.

Many contemporary management books and magazine articles discuss the idea of customer service as essential to success in retail business. A few modern management writers have even developed the concept of employees as customers. The concept relates the principles of customer service to every working relationship within a business organization. Maybe this is the manner in which working relationships should be viewed in your company. Banana thinking would at least have you consider it. The following review of traditional and nontraditional customer relationships will help you gain a better understanding of the concept.

Customer Relationships Within an Organization

A company contains many customer relationships. In the traditional view, an employee performs work for a customer, the supervisor, or the management of a company. But something is missing from this one-way model. In it, employees can choose to work hard, refuse to perform, or in extreme situations, even elect to walk away from their jobs to other places of employment. This makes the management of a company dependent upon the actions of its employees, and in this sense, the employees become the company's customers. The actions employees must take in the performance of their jobs to keep a company profitable therefore makes them customers in the same way that the people purchasing goods from a retail store makes the retailer dependent on them.

You Are Your Supervisor's Customer, As He Is Yours

With this view in mind, you are your supervisor's customer because he or she depends on you to get the job done. And in a reversed sense, your manager is your customer when you expect him or her to trust you to do your work properly and evaluate your performance fairly.

This customer concept can be defined as follows: *A customer is a person whose actions are depended upon by another person.* In other words, if you depend on someone to take some kind of action, you have to think of that person as your customer.

Contractors, service companies, and supply distributors depend on your future relationship as a customer just as you depend on them to perform quality services and to sell you quality products. You depend on some companies for future technological advances in your industry. Therefore, you

135

are a customer to all of your vendors, and they are customers to you.

We All Need One Another

In a broad sense, all employees of a company are customers of each other. This is true because interdependence among employees is necessary to make a company successful. Every employee of an organization needs every other employee. Accountants need technical professionals; marketing personnel need operations service employees; human resource people need sales representatives; front-line supervisors need upper management; and upper management needs the dedication of every employee working for the company. The number of customer relationships within a company is far greater than the number of different working classifications.

Customers and Bananas

Roses are red,
Violets are blue;
If you depend on me,
I'll depend on you.

We both have to grow and perform,
Like separate bananas on a tree;
But we can do it better,
If as a customer is how you look at me.

136

Other Customer Relationships

A host of other customer relationships exist in every segment of our society. When the general public depends on your industry to keep the environment clean, you are their customer. And they are literally your customers, because you depend on them to continue purchasing your products. Members of the U.S. Congress are customers of the citizens of our nation because we depend on them to lead this country wisely. And we are their customers in the sense that they depend on our views to help them form opinions. Possibly the idea of this sort of two-way customer relationship is all that is missing in our political system. Granted, Congress serves citizens, but citizens must also serve Congress for the system to work.

> *Successful marriages are often the result of the willingness, understanding, trust, and compassion that exist in a customer relationship.*

The concept also works in your personal life. When you depend on family members to accomplish a task, they are your customers. The customer/noncustomer relationship is constantly revolving because family members are always depending on each other. Parents are traditionally known as customers to their children. But in the nontraditional sense, children are their parents' customers when their parents depend on them to do their chores. Parents are also their childrens' customers

137

when the children depend on them to teach them wisely. And a husband and wife are constantly changing roles as the customer of each other. So, in accordance with this concept, successful marriages are often the result of the willingness, understanding, trust, and compassion that exist in a customer relationship.

Sometimes we forget how to treat a customer, but successful retailers know how. They cater to the needs of their customers. They try to understand what their customers want, then do whatever it takes to provide it. A successful retail store owner depends on repeat business from customers. If he or she fails to understand and provide what the customer wants, the retail store will most certainly go out of business.

Co-workers as Customers

I once knew a man from Calcutta,
He depended on no one for supper;
So he fixed his own,
Until he was sick and alone,
And he died.

To ensure that we don't end up like the man from Calcutta, we must depend on others. It is effective to enlist the services and assistance of those who want to help us. In so doing we can significantly increase our productivity, while at the same time solidify friendships, family relationships, and work coalitions.

We should take a few lessons from this review of various customer relationships to look at each other as customers in our everyday work. A little more compassion, a little more trust, and just a dash of understanding would help us to be more effec- tive in our inner-company rela- tionships. We often get so caught up in what *we* want, that we for- get the other person may want something too. It all comes down to an "everybody wins" attitude.

> *Think about what you could do for the other person to make him or her to want to work with you again and again.*

To achieve this state of affairs, you must be willing to at least con- sider what the other person wants from a working relationship. It is not that difficult to view another person as a customer. Simply think about what you could do for the other person to make him or her want to work with you again and again. If you put just a little more effort into understanding what your co-workers and supervisors are about, your work relationships will flourish. This is the way of the banana.

If you don't understand your co-worker's attitude or actions, ask him or her a few questions. Maybe you have something in common that would help solidify your work relationship. Be inquisitive. Find out what turns on the people around you. Then turn up the volume and see what happens. You are sure

139

to increase your job enjoyment while improving the disposition of your fellow employees.

Try reading another one of those contemporary business books again. But this time when you get to the part about the customer, look for our parallel meaning, then think about how a specific customer relationship could be applied to where you work. It is likely that you will find a whole new line of literature that can now be applied to your everyday work situation.

Who are the real customers? They are all around you everyday at work.

CHAPTER 12

Active Accountability

"Active Accountability"[1]

Pushing down accountability to the lowest feasible level has caught on across U.S. industry. First-line supervisors and middle managers are now given the authority and responsibility to perform their jobs while being held accountable for results. Yet many companies have failed to thoroughly implement this methodology.

How is it possible to hold people accountable for results when many departments are performing work in the same area of a company?

The question is, "Who is accountable?" Who coordinates work and makes the tough decisions that create an air of risk taking and purpose?

Who has time to communicate the incredible volume of data to different departments and build the multitude of effective working relationships that are required to allow support groups to function?

These matters can be remedied through the proper organizational structure and by fostering real front-line *active accountability*.

The fundamental problem is that many large corporations have been unwilling to substantially increase their spans of control and cut out unnecessary levels of management. This kind of management focuses in on an intermediate staff level where people aren't close to the business. Teamwork and communication are promoted as the means to making the company more effective while utilizing the same ineffective structures. Such an environment isn't conducive to enhancing profits. Nevertheless, all of this works to some extent, though many endeavors fall short.

You have undoubtedly heard it said that, "You must have the right organizational structure to achieve maximum effectiveness." But who is listening? And where is that adventurous spirit that founded many of today's large corporations? Where are the leaders with vision who drive hard to optimize their organizations? There are a few of them out there today who are growing their companies and are achieving uncommon success. But many organizations are still groveling in mediocrity.

> *Where is the adventurous spirit that founded many of today's large corporations?*

Much gets lost in the confusion of multi-departmental accountability. Breakdowns in communication are commonplace when many departments are accountable for work in the same area. And there are many lost opportunities because it takes too long to make a decision. In such an environment the non-risk takers are always willing to throw water on creative fervor.

Support personnel frequently make significant decisions in areas of a company where they have limited experience. They are not close enough to the business to be intuitive, so they are very ineffective because they must analyze everything to the nth degree. And the limited number of people on the front lines continue to make experienced intuitive decisions in a realm that few centrally located employees really understand.

Without active accountability, it is very difficult to stimulate risk taking...

Today's corporate structure designers should be held accountable for the sluggishness of many of today's companies. What is missing is the ability to act fast on opportunities. There aren't enough hours in the day to keep everyone informed and build the multi-departmental relationships that are necessary to succeed. Without active accountability, it is very difficult to stimulate risk taking because many different departments have to be involved in making decisions.

The idea of a central staff of people being more effective than if decentralized is sheer folly. Show me a generalist who is close to the business, and I will show you an individual who can produce several times the work of most centralized staff employees. The closer to the business, the better. Anything else simply doesn't "cut it."

143

The answer to such accountability problems as promoted by many management optimists is to focus on front-line business and reorganize companies into smaller operating entities. The manager of each of the small areas is to then direct all of the business functions in the sector of the company that he or she encompasses. But there should be no overlapping of accountability – the buck has to stop with one person.

> *There should be no overlapping accountability —the buck has to stop with one person.*

Let's define this concept as active accountability. Appropriate accountabilities can still be pushed down to first-line supervisors in such an environment – this is a necessity. But someone close to the business has to be in the driver's seat, or the business gets out of control.

Past management philosophies in American business have established a large number of individual contributors with the title of manager. These outdated business teachings have resulted in an ironclad paradigm of many upper managers in which the number of direct reports to a supervisor can't reach into double digits. And spans of control in the order of twenty-five to fifty and higher are needed to prosper in today's climate.

The primary rationalization for low spans of control is that a manager can't be expected to perform all the administrative duties that come with supervising ten or more employees. But this simply isn't true. A competent manager can handle the administrative duties associated with a sizable number of direct reports. And managers of wide spans of control must work differently from the managers of the past. They must perform few individual contributor tasks, and they must be effective delegators. Through trusting their direct reports to get the job done, and by being well organized, these modern managers can be tremendously effective.

The solutions to accountability problems are directly tied to organizational structure. They will be found by those visionaries who are willing to dissolve the support departments of their companies to increase their span of control of geographical or section asset managers into large exclusive departments. The benefits to large corporations of such management practices would be a significant decrease in complement, increased accountability, increased communications, a focus on the core business, increased effectiveness of employees, and a corresponding increase in profits.

Active accountability and increased spans of control are the deliverers from phlegmatic organization. With the proper leadership and the right people in management positions, companies could utilize these concepts to survive in the competitive world arena. No more operation by committee! No more multi-departmental communication problems! Optimum productivity from people is the objective. We *can* move forward to something mega-effective where active accountability is the rule, and all working associates are empowered to produce peak effectiveness.

The focus of active accountability is not so much the need to expand the span of control of an organization, as it is to decrease the size of the managerial staff. Having too many managers in an organization tends to muddy the waters. It is difficult to establish a common corporate vision with a span of control of less than ten. How can the leader of a corporation expect to create a spirited working atmosphere when hundreds and possibly thousands of tiny empires exist throughout his or her company's structure?

However, if the number of managers can be limited to a ratio of one manager to every twenty workers, the effectiveness of the organization will not be impeded by a lack of unity. It will be strengthened through active accountability. The leader of the company can then directly contribute personal input to the few areas of the organization that are governed by efficient, effective managers who are truly in control of their business units.

"Nobody said it was easy — just possible."

CHAPTER 13

Banana Strategy

We employ strategy during every hour of every day. The very manner in which we solve problems, schedule appointments, prioritize tasks, and perform our daily obligations requires strategy. Companies require strategies to manage their business process flow, and supervisors require strategy to develop employees. Housewives also require strategy to manage their households and to help them schedule time for themselves amid the demands of the family.

There is strategy in many realms. Here are fourteen personal effectiveness strategies that should serve you well.

1. Know every facet of your business.
2. Put forth extra effort into everything you do.
3. Do nothing which is of no use.
4. Worry less and do more.
5. Prioritize.
6. Be persistent in the face of pessimism.
7. Overcome the tendency to spend the majority of your effort on a small percentage of your work.

8. Use it up, wear it out, make it do, or do without.

9. Realize when you have gained, and when you have lost.

10. Get the most for your money.

11. If the shoe fits, wear it.

12. Learn from your failures and fail often.

13. Develop intuition and apply it in all areas of experience.

14. Whatever needs to be done: Do it now.

Know Your Business Well

By far the simplest and most widely used strategy in business is to work hard and get to know your subject well. Hard work pays off, and quality workers know that it takes extra effort to be successful. However, working harder doesn't have to equate to working long hours. It can also mean working smarter.

Knowing your business well is undoubtedly the best way to work smart. If you don't know how to function in every area of your business, you limit yourself. Just imagine the added effectiveness you would enjoy as a financial planner if you understood and were capable of implementing various marketing techniques. Think how much more effective you would be as an engineer or operational manager if you thoroughly understood the accounting side of the business. On the home front, visualize the benefits to a household if a house-spouse were

150

to implement a budget where none existed before. What if the keeper of the house possessed an intimate understanding of the retail grocery business, resulting in the purchase of the highest quality goods at the lowest price?

You don't need to be an expert in every area, merely a person who has experienced several aspects of any specific type of work so you can apply variations to your primary area of expertise. It is not so much a need to be a generalist as it is to be a Jack or Jill of all trades.

Put Forth Extra Effort

Quality work takes extra effort. Extra effort can mean anything from checking to see if you tightened all the lug nuts after changing a flat tire – to double-checking the count on five hundred one dollar bills – to ensuring the validity of the numbers on your corporate balance sheet. There is no substitute for actually taking the time to do a job thoroughly and safely. There is a point where you can be too thorough, which will be discussed in a later chapter. But for now, let's define thoroughness as, "doing what it takes to completely finish a job."

If you are a quality worker then you know when you have completely finished a job. You know that feeling that doesn't hesitate for a moment when signing or engraving your name on the finished product. Sometimes this means working overtime when you are a salaried employee and you know that even though it is not showing up in your paycheck, you

151

still want to turn out a quality product. At other times it simply means thinking through the steps that were taken to get to the finished product in order to ensure that nothing was left out.

Quality Work Takes Extra Effort

If the quality of your work is important to you, then time will not even be a factor with the exception of performing projects in a timely and efficient manner. You will want to take the extra time to do it right, even if it eats into your personal time.

Putting extra effort into personal projects is inherent. We need to put the same effort into our on-the-job performance. So you need to ask yourself, "What would I do differently if I were performing this project for my spouse, my children or grandchildren, or my parents?" Then put the required extra effort into it.

Take ownership of the projects that you perform on the job. Think of them as undertakings that you are personally benefiting from, because that is exactly what is happening. You are getting paid to turn out quality work. And the better the quality, the better the chances are that you will attain your goals.

Do Nothing Which Is of No Use

Another strategy for working smarter is to do nothing which is of no use. This is the cornerstone of the strategy of the Samurai warrior.[1] The definition of a useful activity is as follows: It either teaches you something, puts food on the table, provides shelter, clothes you, provides any other of the necessities of life, soothes you, is an essential element to attaining a goal, is a specific job requirement, or is necessary to sustain life.

We would be amazed if we replaced all of the nonproductive activities of a normal day with only useful ones. It is certain that the productivity of most people would soar astronomically.

A day full of exclusively useful activities would double the effectiveness of some of us, and for others it would mean a quantum leap in productivity. This is such a simple notion – to do only the useful. But I doubt that many of us could perform such a feat...even for an hour. The best that you can strive for is to minimize the number of nonuseful activities in your day.

This could mean shorter telephone conversations. Why spend twenty minutes on the telephone when five will do? Less time visiting with fellow work associates (or in some cases less time daydreaming) would also be an appropriate way to minimize nonuseful time. Also, remember that the shortest route from point A to point B is a straight line, and that you should travel such a line unless it serves some purpose to do otherwise.

Worry Less and Do More

Have you ever considered spending less time daydreaming or worrying about problems? We all worry too much about what we can't affect. This is a very important concept. There are many things in this world that are beyond our control. The flip side of this matter is to not use this idea as a crutch, because very often we are able to do something about a situation that will make a difference. It can be difficult at times to determine what we can and can't affect.

The point to be made here is that it may not be a question of whether or not you can affect a situation as much as whether it really matters if you do. This is often the real issue.

You will find that the majority of the time your worries involve matters that you need to do nothing about; therefore, they are of no use. So when you confront a bothersome situation, give it the "who cares?" test. Ask yourself if there is anyone else in the world who would be bothered with your worry. Then if you can think of only one or two people including yourself, let the majority rule and forget about the trifle that is distressing you.

Worry Is A Time Waster

When you worry, you are typically inactive – you are not doing. You must concentrate on what you are doing today instead of worrying about what you did or didn't do yesterday. If you are not doing, then you are not performing, and this situation in itself leads to ineffectiveness. You have to make the most of your time, and a high percentage of the time, whatever you are worrying about, is not worth the effort; therefore, you are wasting valuable moments. You must minimize this aspect of your being so you can be more effective.

For example, why continually worry about being laid off at your place of employment? The only thing that you can affect with such worry is the quality of your work. If you have done your best, then you should have no regrets, regardless of what the future holds. It may very well be that in habitually worrying about job security, the very thing that makes you a valuable employee could falter – your performance.

So give yourself a break. Be a proponent of the "worry less and do more" strategy. You will be more productive in applying this philosophy, and your level of enjoyment will also escalate.

Prioritize

"Things which matter most should never be at the mercy of the things which matter least," said Goethe. This is such an easy concept, but people from every area of business do a poor job of remembering it.

We all have our pet areas of interest, and it is easy to focus on them only because of personal preference. But being effective in the business world is a little more complicated than focusing on just one thing. Each of us usually have many different matters to juggle at the same time. The secret is to endeavor to prioritize the juggling balls by catching and working on the most important one first, then second, and so on.

It is very important that projects which affect business on a large scale not get put on hold for trivial matters that affect little. An example of this type of behavior would be a worker or supervisor who focuses only on the personality traits of other working associates instead of the business of making money. Another example would be a supervisor who spends two hours discussing how to admonish Joe Blow for a minor traffic accident in a company vehicle when the same decision could have been made in fifteen minutes. Why spend an hour and forty-five minutes on this minor situation when you could have been discussing the innovation of a new corporate money-saving device? Prioritize.

> *Things which matter most should never be at the mercy of the things which matter least.*

There is another important point to be made here. There are many times when you have to be tough as nails to get the job done. You may have to put "the fear of God" into people to instill the importance of meeting a crucial deadline. Use these times sparingly, but when you must, use them. People will certainly understand a few such instances per year. But if this is the way you run your everyday affairs, people won't recognize the *real* urgency in a situation when you need them to see it the most.

Be Persistent

A great woman, my mother, used to tell me, "Don't wear your heart on your sleeve." If I may translate, this means "don't take things so personally." If you are physically unharmed by a thing, then forget about it. Don't dwell on past events that didn't quite turn out as planned, that is with the exception of trying to learn from them.

Don't let unkind words from other people ruin your attitude. Stay in control of your own spirit. I have heard that a man who can rule his spirit is greater than one who can conquer a city. No one but you can make you sad or happy. Only you have control of your emotions and your ultimate performance. So getting even with someone shouldn't even be an option. Endeavor to overcome the verbal cruelty of others by concentrating on improving your own performance. Outshine others by performing – not through vindictiveness or refusing to take action.

Don't dwell on your failures. Remember what you learned from them, then forget the rest. There are many decisions to be made every day. A significant number of these decisions concern whether to keep going or whether to quit. You must endeavor to go forward by trying again instead of moving backward by quitting.

> *Don't let unkind words from other people ruin your attitude.*

You can be very effective through persistence. If you are a person who comes back again and again, you will eventually figure out what it takes to succeed. But if you are a person who quits after a few tries, you are destined for failure.

157

Another Goethe quote is appropriate here: "That which does not kill me makes me stronger." (I think my mother must have known him.)

Don't Spend the Majority of Your Time on a Small Percentage of Your Work

Follow Pareto's Rule

Overcome the tendency to spend the majority of your effort on a small percentage of your work. This principle was devised by a man named Vilfredo Pareto, an Italian economist and sociologist who lived in the late 1800s and early 1900s. He devised what is known today as the *EIGHTY/TWENTY* Rule. The rule says that a business devotes 80 percent of its activity to 20 percent of its product.

The concept is similar to the "trivial many and the critical few" idea that we have already discussed. It is ineffective to spend the majority of your efforts on a small part of your business. There are times when you must focus on a certain segment of the business for a short period, but this should be the exception and not the rule. There needs to be a balance between the work performed and the finished product.

We must endeavor to approach a *FIFTY/FIFTY* Rule in the majority of our business activities. This is good banana thinking. Try to spread your effort and resources throughout your business instead of focusing on only one aspect of the process. In so doing you will minimize wastefulness while ensuring that everyone in your organization is adequately outfitted for success.

Use It Up, Wear It Out, Make It Do, or Do Without

Effectiveness comes from using it up, wearing it out, making it do, or doing without before you buy a new "whatever." Whatever "it" may be, you simply can't afford to replace it, if it is still serviceable. It may not be pretty, and may be old, but don't fix it if it isn't broken.

This basic concept has to do with continuing to use the company equipment at your disposal if it still works. It also says that you must also make an effort to use up the final quantity of a perishable or renewable item before procuring new supplies.

Sometimes you may even find that after you have worn it out, you don't need it anymore. So don't replace the "whatever" just because it was there when you inherited the responsibility for it. Replace it only because you need it to continue making money, to work safely, or to protect the environment.

Assess Gain and Loss

One of the most important aspects of surviving in today's world is judgment. To be effective you must be a good judge of when you have gained and when you have lost. This concept applies across the board with respect to money concepts, family matters, work on individual projects, and affairs of the heart.

You have to know when you have gained, so you can continue to do whatever it was that resulted in success. You have to know when you have lost, so you can improve and try again or simply avoid the type of action or behavior that resulted in the loss. This concept differs from the one having to do with persistence because there will occasionally be times when you discover that you want no part of a matter once you have confronted it. Sometimes this is wise, and sometimes it is not. You have to be the judge.

If you are a person who is good at judging gain and loss, you will build an impressive portfolio of wins, and the additive effect will be prosperity. But if you are one of those many individuals who can't tell the difference between the two, you will inevitably end up with very little to show for your work, i.e., $1 + 1 + 1 + 1 = 4$, but $1 - 1 + 1 - 1 = 0$.

Get the Most for Your Money

Another good strategy to be implemented in your business or personal life is that of getting the most for your money. This may seem an overly simple concept, but we are often unwilling to take risks on a regular basis in order to obtain the best deal. So one way to implement this strategy is to purchase used equipment and other used goods when available instead of buying new.

Let someone else buy the new cars or new office furniture at inflated prices. When you buy new goods, you are throwing away the monetary difference between the new and used price. There is a time when you should buy new, but there are many other times when whatever you are purchasing will fill a need just as well if it is used.

There is a substantial payout in buying used equipment. Applying this concept to the used car market should give you a better appreciation of purchasing used instead of new.

Let someone else buy the new cars or new office furniture at inflated prices.

Wouldn't you rather pay half price for your next automobile? You can do so by purchasing a higher end luxury sedan that is a few years old. Suppose for example that you spend $30,000 on a new car and then sell it in four years for the sum of $15,000. In simplified terms that comes out to $3,750 a year (not including interest or the time value of money). New automobiles depreciate the most in the first four years; therefore, when you buy a new car and drive it for forty-eight months, you are being hit with the largest depreciation burden during the life of the car.

If you purchased a four-year-old vehicle for $15,000, spent another $1,000 on maintenance, then sold it in two years for $12,000, you would be spending only $2,000 a year for a vehicle that is still very serviceable.

You can do this today with many used European automobiles because they experience significant depreciation during the first four years, then hold their value very well thereafter. All you have to do is study the market, learn about a specific item of interest, form a strategy, then implement your low-cost purchase of used items.

There are also occasions when limited service or off-brand products are the thing to buy in lieu of new or used name-brand items. Take a VCR for example. After five to ten years of service, VCRs literally wear out. Why pay $150 for a used unit that will never work properly when you could purchase a new Slamwung unit for $200, which is still half the price of a brand-name VCR?

However, in the case of a widget machine, the avenue to take may be to purchase the used one that is ten years old because it is better built. When refurbished, it will cost half as much as a new one and will possibly require fewer repairs, this is the way to go.

You have to be careful with this strategy because many times a used unit is not as energy efficient as a newer model. So do your homework. There is an apples-to-apples cost comparison in this case to be made. If you are unsure concerning the energy efficiency of the type and model of used equipment you are purchasing, have some tests run to determine the same. Better yet, have the entire unit inspected by an expert if you are unsure about its condition or present performance capabilities.

This brings up an important issue: when do you pay for an inspection by an expert, and when do you forgo it? Of course the cost of the used item and your level of expertise should govern the need for inspection. You would be unwise to pay for the inspection of a $100 piece of equipment when the inspection costs $50 and the price of a new model is $200. The best bet would be to take a risk that the $100 piece of equipment is in good working condition or ask for a demonstration (if possible) before you purchase it.

You would be justified in paying $500 to an expert for inspecting a used piece of machinery that is priced at $100,000. But if your level of expertise on the aforementioned equipment was such that you could make a judgment call concerning its condition, then by all means you would be wise to save yourself the $500.

An analogous situation is that of the inspection of a used home by a structural specialist. Such inspections are performed today on a routine basis before the completion of a home purchase agreement. Many of us don't have the expertise to know what to look for in order to evaluate the state of a given house. So as the purchaser of a used home, we demonstrate good business sense by hiring an inspector to evaluate what we can't, before we finalize the deal. In the case of a new house, building codes and city inspectors fill this requirement.

You have to know much about a product to be an effective new, used, and off-brand comparison shopper. You also have to be willing to accept a little risk, fewer or no guarantees, not quite as pretty an item, fewer bells and whistles, and in the case of used equipment, slightly less than perfect working condition: but at a whole lot cheaper cost. Now that's making the most effective use of your money. But you must do everything you can to ensure that the performance of used or off brand equipment can be sustained at an acceptable level for a reasonable period of time.

Be careful about being lured into the "new is better" sales pitch.

The savings afforded through buying used items can greatly increase your standard of living or level of service to your customers over those who are not willing to take reasonable risks. So be careful about being lured into the "new is better" sales pitch. New equipment is new for a while, but after a few months it is used in every sense of the word.

Buying used is simply more cost effective if you buy smart and observe the following guidelines:

1. Be careful not to pay as much for used as you would for new – sometimes you would be better off buying a new limited-service product or an off brand.

2. Make sure what you are buying is in good working condition, or know your subject well enough that you can repair an inoperable item and still come out way ahead of a new purchase.

3. Have a used item inspected by an expert if you are unsure of its condition.

4. Compare prices with other used goods to purchase the best deal.

164

5. Be willing to accept a few scratches, fewer conveniences, and moderately lower performance when purchasing used equipment.

6. Refurbish a used item only if required, and don't make the mistake of attempting to turn the old into new.

My sixth recommendation leads to another important concept: "Don't try to make old things new." It is okay to refurbish an item to make it serviceable again, just remember that an old car is going to be an old car no matter how much glitz you put on it. Learn to live with its creaks and small problems. Go ahead and try to make it look, feel, smell, and perform like it is brand new. And be satisfied that it fulfills your basic transportation needs at a good price, which is hopefully the reason you bought it in the first place. But if you want it to be in completely new condition, then buy a new car.

There are opportunities to have your cake and eat it too with respect to the purchase of used equipment. Occasionally you may be lucky enough to come across an opportunity to buy a used item that looks and performs like new. In these instances you should by all means make the deal and even pay a little extra if required.

If the Shoe Fits, Wear It

Many of us search our whole lives for one thing that we can do well. So when we find it, we should cherish it and keep developing the gift of our talent until the day we die.

165

I once knew a person who could paint beetles incredibly well. Yes, beetles...as in bugs. He was a master and didn't even realize it. His talent was incredible. His paintings would look just like photographs of the real thing. They were accurate in every detail. The only problem was, there wasn't any market for his beetle art. He assumed that *National Geographic* published only photographs of animals. But I doubt that he ever sent one of his paintings to them to find out if that was really the case. So he quit painting, and to this day, he hasn't picked up another brush.

Such a waste of talent. The creation of such beauty is a gift. It is not a matter of dollars and cents. It is a matter of doing what you do well, then taking your abilities to the limit. Our beetle painter should have continued painting because someday he would have likely found appreciation for his accomplishments, especially when it was done so expertly.

The real problem was that this person wished he had musical talent, and he had very little. He focused on collecting musical memorabilia and being an audiophile instead of doing and creating what he was really good at. He found it difficult to devote himself to one thing and take that thing as far as his abilities would allow.

But he had another alternative. He could have transferred his talent for painting beetles to something else if he felt it wasn't productive to continue painting bugs. Perhaps there was a modern-day Rembrandt or Van Gogh waiting to emerge from this person, and all he needed to do was to take a fork in the road of creative discovery to find his true capabilities.

Whatever it is that you do well, you should continue to do it. If it is painting, then pick up the brush often. If it is repairing automobiles, then keep the wrenches handy. If it is singing, then open your mouth and serenade the world. Only by determining what you are good at, then focusing on it, can you achieve maximum effectiveness in at least one discipline.

You need to experience all forms of creativity, but there are not enough hours in a lifetime to learn how to do everything in an expert manner. Therefore, you must wear out that shoe when it fits, then get it resoled if necessary so you can continue your contribution to the world in an area in which you excel.

Learn How to Fail

We have discussed this point in a previous chapter, but it is such an important point that I feel it is imperative to reiterate here, as I will again in the next chapter.

You must learn how to fail. In doing so, you gain new knowledge and understanding of what it is you are attempting to accomplish. You must fail and fail often if you are to gain knowledge, all of which is a prerequisite to achieving a high level of effectiveness. You must then continue to fail in new areas as you expand your effectiveness to encompass other subjects and disciplines.

Intuitive Effectiveness

True effectiveness is not having to think about the solution to a problem. It is when the solution is inherent. Intuitive effectiveness is knowing a subject so well that you don't have to ponder or ask for a second opinion. You can simply answer questions and solve problems in your area of expertise as soon as they are perceived or presented.

Dealing with situations will be elementary when you make use of intuitive effectiveness. When you attain such effectiveness, your mind becomes the incredible processor that it was meant to be. You become a lean, mean thinking machine and there will be few obstacles that require more than a few seconds of reflection.

(I have devoted Chapter 15 to the subject of intuitive risk taking, which includes more on the concept of intuitiveness and how to use it to become more effective.)

Learn the Benefits of
Problem Solving and Doing it Now

There is considerable strategy that can be used in problem solving. Solving a small problem can be relatively easy, but often when we are presented with a complicated problem it is hard to figure out where to start. The following is an approach that has been developed to help solve large problems.

 168

The first thing you must do with a large problem is to simplify it. This can be done in two ways. You can split the problem into smaller parts, then solve each part. Or you can negate the parts of the problem to the point where you get to a basic ingredient.

Take for example the building of an airplane. There are many different segments that engineers and designers work on independently before they are brought together to construct an actual flying machine. The manufacture of the complete, complicated device is the result of a multitude of smaller projects brought together with a common, overall objective.

Solving your own complicated problems is very similar to building an airplane. First, you have to split the problem into several elemental parts, solve each section independently, then mesh the results back together into a final solution.

Insignificant parts of a problem can often be negated as a prelude to your final solution. This method of problem solving usually works best in areas where 90 percent accuracy is acceptable. Sending a man to the moon wouldn't be one of these examples. There was no room for error in the Apollo program. But such intricate problem solving is the exception, not the rule. Most business situations give you much more room to negate the unnecessary.

The simplification of a problem is a judgment call on the part of the problem solver. If you can learn to simplify the majority of your problems, you

169

can be incredibly effective. Complicated projects that require hours, days, or weeks must be planned, prioritized, and performed as your schedule permits. But as far as your smaller tasks that require little time to complete are concerned, you should be an advocate of the "do it now" philosophy.

You must be flexible to allow for impromptu tasks that arise during the course of a normal day. To do so, you may be required to put your present work on hold to spend a brief period of time on a short memorandum or a consultation with a work associate. You will be much more efficient and productive if you will take five to ten minutes to do it now instead of waiting until later. This will also ensure that a minor task will not be forgotten.

Hyper Life and 90 Percent Accuracy

Time management is a very important part of developing an effective overall business strategy. It is amazing how much you can fit into a day. Think of the busiest day you have ever experienced. Think of all the things you accomplished during that day. Then ask, "Why was I so productive?" Was it because you planned in advance? Was it because you had additional determination, or was it merely because you got a good night's sleep?

You should endeavor to gain an understanding of the relationship between cause and effect. Think about what you did differently to make something happen better than it happened the last time you did it. Then try to follow a new path to do it better the next time, and the time after that. What you will find is that if you develop the energy and motivation to plan ahead, that you can achieve much more than you thought during every day.

You may not have ready access to all of the answers when making a business decision. A window of opportunity may pass you by if you take the time to attempt to uncover the last answer or morsel of data. And it is you who have to determine when enough data has been gathered to make the final decision. Often, the majority of facts concerning a matter can be gathered quickly without a major study or lengthy investigation. But the additional 10 to 20 percent of the information may take twice as long to obtain.

So go with the 90 percent of information that can be gathered, or miss out on the plan. You can be effective when making the majority of your decisions based on gathering only 90 percent of the available data. It is ineffective to spend the additional time and effort to gather the other 10 percent of the information that is required to make a fool-proof decision. Why? Because no decision is without risk. You are the fool if you think effectiveness comes from taking twice as long to perform a project because you are unwilling to take a calculated risk. Effectiveness comes from performing a maximum amount of work in a minimum amount of time.

One last word of advice concerning strategy. Cram your day full of life stuff. This is your life, and you have command of it. If you don't get done what you intended today, then you have no one to blame but yourself. You alone control your output and success.

Call this proactivity, or merely self-guidance. Have fun with it. Make your day's chores a game. You can keep score by seeing how much you accomplished today, then determining how to accomplish more tomorrow, and more the next day. Once you have figured out how to be very productive, you will have to figure out how to maintain this high level of effectiveness – and that is almost as difficult as discovering how to manage your time in the first place. Nobody said it was easy – just possible.

Make your day's chores a game.

Life itself can be a breeze, or you can struggle through every minute of every day. It is somewhere between the two where effectiveness is found. Often, you have a choice of which avenue to travel. The easy path to immediate self-gratification leads to a future of mediocrity. The path of the thinker, doer, questioner, of the habitual student, leads to personal satisfaction and success.

The latter requires persistence and fortitude which exists in us all. We have to study, try, and fail, and study, try, and fail until we get it right. And then when we have achieved the best that we can muster today, we must question whether it is good enough when we awake tomorrow.

There is additional strategy to be learned in attitude, dress, posture, confrontation, conversation, and in many other areas. However, the way of the habitual student is the only true universal strategy. It is one that all men and women should heed and apply. It is the way of the banana thinker – the only way to discover and sustain true effectiveness.

PART III
Bananas at Play

CHAPTER 14

Baseball and Bananas

Otto the gorilla loves to play. We already know about the enjoyment he experiences as he spends his days swinging limb to limb through the trees. He has no worries about salary, mortgage payments, or what clothes he is going to wear today. What a wonderful life he must lead, living solely for the purpose of eating, sleeping, and playing.

As we discussed in the first chapter, a gorilla family sometimes literally devours a banana tree when they are feeding. They thoroughly enjoy this ritual, and besides providing their entertainment for the day, it supplies roughage in their diet. It must give them such a sense of power over their environment to know they can vanquish a mighty banana tree. And it must add to their pleasure after literally tearing the thing to shreds, to not have to clean up the disheveled plaything when they're done.

Oh, how they play, and though it may seem to us a preposterous notion, Otto knows about baseball. He uses the whole banana tree for a bat, and a handful of bananas for balls. He reduces the tree to one mighty stalk, then uses it to smash the bananas into the ground. There are no bases, no umpires, and few spectators. There is only the pure unadulterated joy of a gorilla as he performs his own adaptation of the game. It is baseball without any rules. It is unfettered fun in the form of eating, doing, and living for the sake of play.

Just as Otto understands his variation of the game, we must also understand our own baseball amusement. Whether it is a conventional mode of baseball, or one we have made up for our own enjoyment, we must adapt ourselves and learn to play the game.

There are times when there is more to being an observer than just sitting and watching a game. Take professional baseball for example, there is such culture and frolic built around the contest. Participative playing should always be first preference, but attending and observing a professional baseball game is much more than spectating. It involves a participation at several basic levels at the same time. There is something about watching baseball that feeds our primal need to observe and join people collectively having fun.

Baseball as We Know It

A baseball stadium is a wonderful setting. It is a place where dreams become reality for children and where grownups remember their youth.

I can still taste the hot dogs, peanuts, popcorn, and soft drinks. The billboards on the outfield fence are forever etched in my mind's eye, and the light scent of tobacco smoke fills my nostrils. The cheers of my fellow observers are overpowering, and I am drawn into the game. The batter hits the ball deep along the foul line into left field for a double, and I am the first to cheer. I stand shouting the slugger's nickname as he slides into second base. "Great hit!" I shout, as the successful slugger rises from the dirt.

What is it about baseball that is so uplifting? Young boys come to know heroes, and old men sit by the radio reminiscing about players of yesterday. Could it be that we know the game so well that it is something we can depend on in an almost unmanageable world? Could it be that we trust the world of baseball to be there season after season more than we trust our own manner of play? Or could it be that we can escape into a baseball game for a few hours at a time – remembering how timeless is the heritage that made baseball what it is today?

Banana thinking and baseball are similar in many ways. All baseball players step up to the plate with the hope of making the almost perfect bat-to-ball connection that literally "peels the cover off of the ball" as it sails into the stratosphere.

> *Only by batting time and time again can we increase our percentage of hits.*

This is very similar to peeling those bananas from the bottom. When we are coming up with ideas, no matter how preposterous, we are standing in the batter's box, swinging the bat. But unlike a batter, we have an infinite number of chances to take before we strike out.

One trend that is destined for failure and monotony is refusing to step into the batter's box. In so doing we never put ourselves at risk; therefore, we rarely make any progress or experience any excitement. Excitement is the real meaning of the game. It is what happens when our play reaches a heightened and very satisfying level. We like normal, lethargic, steady-as-she-goes play, but we crave unusual, exciting, hold-on-to-your-seats action in which we are an active participant.

If we keep swinging the bat, sooner or later we are bound to come up with a hit – an exciting idea. But only by batting time and time again can we increase our percentage of hits. In so doing we are destined for many short-term failures, but we should receive our failures with enthusiasm and learn from them. Each hit we make is like generating a new idea. Some players are happy with a single, some are in search of their one thousandth double, and others are in the hunt for a bases-loaded grand slam.

We must participate in the game if we are to fulfill our desire to have fun.

Whatever the case, they all keep batting with the eternal hope to get more hits. They realize they must continue to step into the batter's box to be successful. Time after time they fail to produce, but they keep on swinging, keep on trying.

We could learn from observing our persistent baseball heroes. They teach us that if we keep playing, success is always just a few hits away. They are very happy with a .300 batting average, which means that seven out of ten times they come to bat they fail to get on base. How marvelously they must live their lives with this persistent attitude. They know that all they have to do to be successful is keep playing hard and to keep on trying.

To draw a parallel, life is like a perpetual baseball game. We must be persistent, and we must keep playing. We must participate in the game if we are to fulfill our desire to have fun. Being a spectator is ineffectual. Actively playing our favorite game is much more rewarding.

Play the Game!

What about the way in which we play? As young children we were concerned only about playing the game. We didn't worry too much about keeping score, and we certainly didn't lose any sleep over whether we won or lost. It was better if you won, but simply being allowed to play the game is what was important. So we were content to cavort with minimal equipment, make up our own rules, and play until the earth rotated our field of frolic into unseeable, unplayable darkness.

> *...we must endeavor to do it from a child's perspective....*

As adults we are concerned about following conventional rules and competition. We are so concerned about winning, that we often forget that having fun was the reason we got involved in the first place. And because many adults look at play in

181

the same way that they look at work, it is viewed as being less useful than could otherwise be the case.

When we play, we must endeavor to do it from a child's perspective and make having fun our number one priority. If the rules get in the way, we should make up new rules. If other people involved in our activity get too serious about the aspect of play, we should find another arena in which to frolic.

You should play for the sake of having fun — with no other reason to detract from your enjoyment.

Stress liberation is one of the primary benefits of play. Play is necessary to overcome everyday stressors. I laugh to myself every time I hear the name Plato (play-toe) because (I tell myself flippantly) this has to be a pen name. He wrote in so many different ways to "live your life for the sake of play," that I have to assume he was playing with his name.

Play must be an integral part of our lives. We must live to play every hour of every day. Our work can be more fun if we play at it, our families can be more enjoyable if we play with them, and our lives in general will be far more fulfilling if — like our friend Otto — we take the time to play.

"Playing it safe protects what you have today, but it erodes creativity which makes it impossible to be the best of the best tomorrow."

CHAPTER 15

Intuitive Risk Taking

isk taking is an important part of life. If you take too few risks, it is likely you will enjoy life less than those who jump from one risk-taking situation to another. If you are a poor risk-taker, it is very likely that you will live meagerly compared to a good risk-taker.

But if you can overcome the fear of failure and prioritize your risks, half the battle is won. If you can incorporate intuition and experience into risk-taking situations, the equation is complete. True banana thinking is an important choice when the situation calls for it.

That reminds me of my Dairy Queen story. Approximately ten years ago I went to a Dairy Queen brazier food restaurant to order and carry out a meal and treats for my wife and another couple who was visiting. It was an uneventful day until I entered the Dairy Queen.

I stood in line for a very short period of time, then I ordered several hamburgers, a hot dog, french fries, two sundaes, two shakes, and a few other miscellaneous items. Before the cashier could ring up

"Whether it is a conventional mode of baseball,
or one that we have made up for our own
enjoyment, we must adapt ourselves and
play the game."

the total, I blurted out $17.68, and – you guessed it – the cash register rang up a total of $17.68. The cashier was astounded at my intuitiveness, and I was even a little impressed myself.

Maybe I had unconsciously added up the items in my mind, but the feeling was different from that. It was as if all of a sudden the number was in my head and I just had to get it out. I won't try to make any more out of the incident than that. But it did get me thinking about the sort of intuitive, or, "hunch" thinking that we often hear so much about. I quickly paid for the food, took a number, then sat down in a booth facing the counter and the kitchen waiting for my order to be prepared.

Perhaps my math skills were incredibly heightened as I readied to pay my bill. Maybe God spoke the information to me to let me know there is more than mere sensory knowledge to be reckoned with in this life. Or perhaps I simply lucked out when speaking the price. I am uncertain as to what it was. The point is, I am reminded of the event every time I intuitively "feel" the solution to a problem, rather than using a conventional problem-solving technique. A few years later I experienced a similar event while playing a simple children's game with my brother.

> *If you can overcome the fear of failure and prioritize your risks, half the battle is won.*

When I was a child, I was taught a game called slapjack. It is a very simple game that anyone old enough to slap the table can play. A deck of cards is split up into equal parts, and each player gets his equitable share. The point of the game is to end up with all of the cards. Each player turns over his cards on a common area of a table until a jack is revealed, then the first person to slap the jack wins it and all of the cards beneath it.

After several times through the deck, an experienced slapjack player has a good idea of when the jacks are due to come up. It is something he learns from experience, as well as how to hold his hand to achieve the quickest slap possible. There is also a certain strategy involved in turning over the cards. If he turns them over too slowly, his opponent will see the card before he does, and if it is a jack, he will know it is time to strike.

The interesting thing about the game of slapjack is that when a person plays it a lot and knows what he is doing, he has the edge over his opponent. He intuitively knows when the jacks are coming, and, therefore, he knows when to be ready to slap, which greatly increases his chance of winning. Experience has everything to do with it.

On one particular occasion, I was playing a game of slapjack with my brother Terry. We split the cards and started playing. After about six or seven minutes into the game, I had slapped three jacks, and he had slapped none.

My brother was running out of cards quickly, so I was preparing for absolute victory. I had already played all of my cards and had restacked them to

188

continue the game. Terry had only three cards left, and I knew that one of them was a jack because I had already seen the others played. And then it happened – my brother turned over the first of his three cards and before it hit the table I said to myself that it was a six of clubs. The card fell to the table, and it was indeed a six of clubs.

Terry turned over his next card and in a similar fashion I said to myself, "This card is the queen of diamonds." And that is what was revealed. At this point my mind was reeling, and I knew the next card had to be a jack. My brother flipped it over, and my hand came down on it swiftly to end the game. Terry looked at me in amazement wondering how anyone could have such quick reflexes. Of course, it wasn't my reflexes at all that won the game, it was my paying attention to what had already been played.

The "hunch" a detective may have in solving a criminal case, or the kind of intuition you may experience in winning the bid on a business deal, will often come into play because of paying attention. The detective watches for clues. So should we. When we do, we can *think ahead*.

I believe my slapjack experience was simply one of those times similar to the Dairy Queen incident in which everything fell into place and my subconscious calculated the outcome. But this is what I believe, and there is still that unknown factor. The answer to it all may always remain a mystery to me, but some answers to some of your questions

189

concerning luck, intuition, and experienced speculation are contained in this chapter.

So there you have it: Intro 101 to intuitive risk taking. By now you should be asking yourself the following question: "Intuitive risk taking, is it supernatural or is it based on experience and reason?" I hope the following will help you gain a little understanding on the matter of this often misunderstood subject. If you can learn how to utilize intuition, knowledge, and experience as part of risk taking, you will gain an advantage in your personal life and in business over those who refuse to take reasonable risks. Banana thinkers take risks.

The Way of the Banana Involves Intuitive Risks

Intuitive risks are taken every day by highly successful banana thinkers. The majority of these high achievers have mastered the art of risk taking and understand the importance of listening to their intuition. So the rest of us must be missing something. Could it be possible that we don't understand the diverse aspects of risk taking? Is it also possible that we don't fully comprehend the effectiveness of using intuition to solve problems? Yes, it is.

> *Playing it safe protects what we have today, but it erodes creativity....*

Most of us have discovered that if we consistently play it safe, we end up in a mediocre soup. Playing it safe protects what we have today, but it erodes creativity that makes it impossible to be the best of the best tomorrow.

The consequence of avoiding risks is a sluggish lifestyle that eventually consumes us in monotony. Both of the big Ms (mediocrity and monotony) apply to intuitive risk taking. They may be the mainstay of your life, but you don't have to stay there. The following fifteen points will help you move along from there.

Fifteen Points to Remember in Understanding Intuitive Risk-Taking

1. Look for fewer assurances.
2. Be willing to accept failure as a prelude to success.
3. Listen to your intuition. It can be your guide to extraordinary productivity.
4. Be willing to speculate on your intuition.
5. Take large risks only when there is a reasonable chance of success.
6. Risk primarily in areas where you have personal experience.
7. Take small risks in areas of low experience and accept failure to gain seasoning.
8. Be self-confident in your ability to make decisions.
9. Since there may be no second chance, take the reasonable risk now.
10. Be less thorough – don't retreat to analysis.
11. Understand that obstacles are opportunities to win.

191

12. Significantly increase your chance of success by setting many risk-taking events in motion.

13. Remember that success is directly proportional to the number of chances taken.

14. Confront situations that cause you to feel fear.

15. Understand that by risking yourself you are truly experiencing life.

Excitement and Motivation

There are many people in the world who long for excitement in their lives. But they lack motivation and have probably never known how to find it. If you are one of them, excitement through risk taking can be your motivation.

Risking Failure

Many people look for too many assurances when considering a risk-taking situation. The dictionary defines the word *risk* as the possibility of loss or failure. Failure is not a dirty word.

An individual's failure scorecard is a measure of his willingness to take risks. Failures are valuable experiences that keep us on the path to success. Progress is made by men and women who are not afraid to fail as long as success is on the horizon.

Banana Thinkers Take Reasonable Risks

Risk taking is an acquired skill that is made possible through experience and sustaining the proper attitude. Either a person has the attitude to take risks or he doesn't. True banana thinkers understand this attitude. They know there has to be a level of uncertainty in any risk-taking endeavor. Their sincerity is reflected in a willingness to gamble on intuition. Many of them are willing to risk whatever it takes in an all-out effort to succeed.

Knowing when not to take risks is the most dubious part of risk taking. This is usually where the fainthearted find it easy to say no and walk away to safer interests. Discriminating risk takers enlist experience and intuition to help them evaluate every risk-taking opportunity as a potential win or loss. This is the way of the banana.

My definition of reasonable risk taking is: ***Risking what you can afford to lose in any endeavor with a reasonable chance of success.*** So generally, if the chance to win is not greater than the alternative, risk yourself elsewhere. Of course, there will always be instances where determining the chance for success is not possible. When this is the case, you must rely solely on your instincts.

> *Risk taking is risking what you can afford to lose in any endeavor with a reasonable chance of success.*

In many risk-taking endeavors there is no second chance once the opportunity has passed by. You will rarely be sorry if you take the risk, give it your best, and still don't attain your goals. On the other hand, you will be dismayed every time you reflect on yesterday and wish you could do it over again because this time you would take the chance. You will lead a more satisfying life if you confront the fear of failure and pursue every opportunity to take reasonable risks.

Self-Confidence and Intuition

Intuition is a matter of self-confidence. There is no obstacle that can stand in your way if you have it. Confidence in your decision-making abilities gives you an advantage because you know the majority of your risk taking will be successful. If you are an informed, experienced, and confident person, then you need only to understand your intuition to be a good risk taker.

> *Your intuition is merely the subconscious mind making thousands of split-second comparisons and judgments in an effort to help you make the right decision.*

Most people need to have more of an appetite for uncertified results. Most of the time if you feel it strongly enough, then there are underlying reasons why your intuition says, "Just risk it." Think about the people you perceive to be the most effective performers. It is likely they are people who "feel" their way through problems instead of retreating to analysis. So listen to your intuition. It can be your guide to extraordinary productivity.

194

Experienced people arrive at a point in their lives where they are so familiar with their environment, they can often feel the solution to a problem. There are many who would ridicule this type of quick decision-making ability. They would call it taking a short-cut instead if putting forth real effort to do a job right. But that is simply not true. The reality of the matter is that a subject is often known well enough by an experienced person that the answers to problems associated with it are inherent. It is having to explain to the analyzers why an intuitive decision was made that leads to ineffectiveness.

There is nothing magical about intuition. Your intuition is merely the subconscious mind making thousands of split-second comparisons and judgments in an effort to help you make the right decision. All you have to do is listen. There will be times when you can't justify your answer to a question or solution to a problem. So why try? *Consider all things, analyze nothing, and try to "feel" everything.*

Too Thorough to Be Effective

Perfectionist behavior is an affliction caused by an unwillingness to take risks. Perfectionists investigate every detail until at last they know all about a situation. Their final decision is based entirely on known facts and substantiated research. This level of thoroughness is appropriate if you are working for NASA or building an artificial heart. But the majority of work requires a much simpler approach.

195

Experienced people should gather a moderate amount of data, rely on their instincts, then make a decision in a short period of time. Then they can get on with the rest of their work which very likely requires that many more decisions be made. It is possible to be very productive by applying this philosophy. Remember the advice that you once received, "Your first answer to a question on a test is your best answer." The same principle applies here.

We have to be self-regulating. We have to set our own boundaries and know how far we can push beyond them. From experience each of us must know when we did not do our homework and made too many mistakes, compared to when we did just enough work to perform an above average job in record time – that is effectiveness.

Game Playing

Game playing is an important component of risk taking. A player evaluates a game of chance using past experience and then trusts his intuition to help him make quick, accurate decisions. You can acquire an understanding of this process by investigating different types of game playing and determining what it takes to be successful.

In some games of chance the odds of winning are less than 50 percent. So you might ask the question, "If the overall odds are not in my favor, how can I expect to win?" The answer to that question is part of the challenge of game-playing. You can be successful if you capitalize on winning streaks, conserve your resources, and know when to walk away. And these skills can only be developed through experiencing various game-playing situations and determining what it takes to be successful.

My experiences in the game of Monopoly are a good example of intuitive risk taking. When I was much younger, I thoroughly learned the rules of the game. I often played Monopoly with the kids in my neighborhood. I would end up winning the majority of the time simply because I had the most experience and the best knowledge of the game. In fact, I knew it so well that I could tell anyone where his token would end up on the board before he had even counted the spots on the dice.

To this day when I play Monopoly with my sons, I still remember what houses and hotels cost on Boardwalk and Park Place, or any other real estate on the board. Knowing what to expect at any turn in the game allows me to take more calculated risks. And with those risks there has always been more opportunity to win.

There are three lessons that you will discover from studying game playing. Be an informed risk taker, limit your exposure time to the same risk because your luck will eventually run out, and always make sure you have a good chance of success. Of course the chance of success will never be 100 percent, or it wouldn't be called risk taking.

Game playing can be very rewarding, but never risk what you can't afford to lose. The same concept applies to your everyday life. Never put it all on the line. However, you should put just enough out there versus a substantial reward to make the risk worth taking. You may fail several times in similar risk situations before you gain enough experience to reverse the trend and start winning. So risk small amounts while you are learning, and save the big speculation for experienced endeavors. A primary part of risk taking is the knowledge that one big gain cancels out many losses. However, you should be aware of your inevitable defeat if you persist against odds that are not in your favor.

When you become an experienced game player, you may occasionally encounter a long winning streak during which you may feel that you can exert your will on the game. But if you try to analyze this concept, you will discover that it is confidence and intuition that helped you win. It is confidence that you have done your homework and have played enough to experience most of the obstacles, thereby giving your intuition a basis from which to function.

Luck and Timing

The phrase "a very lucky person" is often used as a reference to someone who is an effective risk taker. Luck is not an abstract, uncontrollable quantity. People who are lucky are doing something right, and unlucky people are doing something wrong. People who are in a continual state of calamity are in discord with their surroundings, and they are often not paying attention to their current situation. Very lucky people are the ones who consider most of their options. They look before they leap and are good at life in general because they seek to work in harmony with their surroundings.

Lucky people are typically well prepared and often possess a keen sense of timing. Timing is very important because if you push an idea at just the right time, you can be very successful. If your timing is off, you can fail miserably. Timing may be the most complex ingredient of luck and risk taking. Few people have natural timing, most of us have to practice hard to attain a high level of timing coordination. A sense of timing can be developed only through experiencing many risk-taking situations.

> *Timing may be the most complex ingredient of luck and risk taking.*

Persistence is also related to timing. Lucky people fail from time to time, but they keep on trying until they succeed. People who are in the right place at the right time are said to have good timing. But these people are simply putting forth extra effort into encompassing as many matters as possible. They are active people who have discovered that success is directly proportional to the number of chances taken.

To sum up this line of thinking, it could best be said that lucky people are the ones who possess the traits that are necessary to succeed. They are experienced risk takers who set many events in motion that ultimately result in many successful outcomes.

One last thought on luck: luck is the absence of fear. When you are not afraid to risk failure, you can expect to be exceptionally lucky.

199

Overcoming Obstacles

What a dull world it would be if there were no obstacles to overcome. Banana thinkers look at obstacles as opportunities to win. Don't look at them in any other way. You can win or you can try again, but you can never lose if you keep trying. Long-term losses are almost inconceivable when you are persistent and have confidence.

Your biggest obstacle is fear. So confront those situations that cause you to feel fear, and in dealing with them, you will find new confidence and strength that can be used in future encounters. If you are afraid of a thing, choose to learn more about it and commit yourself to overcoming that fear. Most likely you are afraid of situations that involve taking risks in areas where you have little experience. Whether it is the fear of flying, of the water, of public speaking, or simply the fear of failure, you can overcome it through education, practice, and persistence. In so doing you will gain the experience needed to nourish your self-confidence and intuition.

> *Lucky people fail from time to time, but they keep trying until they succeed.*

A Personal Obstacle

I must share with you a continuing obstacle in my life that I chose to overcome.

Several years ago I decided to take an introductory flight in a glider. During that flight I was inspired, and afterwards I decided to become a glider pilot.

When I first started soaring lessons, I was very afraid of being in full control of what could be the instrument of my death. So I worked hard and took many practice flights – building each time on what I had previously achieved. Eventually, I overcame my anxiety and improved to the degree that I became a licensed glider pilot.

> *Obstacles are opportunities to win.*

Now, before each flight I am still afraid. I am afraid of not being able to control the aircraft if the weather suddenly turns dangerous while I am floating in mid-air. The moment I slip into the cockpit I can feel my foot quivering on the rudder pedal, and I tell myself that I can do it about a hundred times.

The sense of being alive is magnified in those few minutes before I take off. So I summon all of my concentration, and I focus on the skills that I have learned which allow me to safely pilot the glider. I simply refuse to let fear stop me from flying.

Piloting a glider is an exhilarating experience. It is an extreme situation that requires utter concentration and accurate decision-making ability. I find that my greatest reward in flying is not in the flight itself, but in what happens after I glide gracefully to the ground.

After each flight I have an incredible feeling of satisfaction, and I revel in the sensation of having mastered my fears. My confidence has peaked, and

I have a sense of accomplishment that is awe inspiring.

I view soaring as the consummate test of my decision-making skills and my ability to deal with extreme situations. I frequently tell myself that a difficult task is easy compared to piloting a glider. Each new gliding experience helps me keep motivated until I have an opportunity to take the next adventure.

By overcoming similar obstacles in your life, you will be developing the courage to stay calm in difficult situations. At the same time you will be fine tuning your ability to make decisions in extreme circumstances. Overcoming obstacles will provide you with the experience and self-confidence required to take additional risks.

Accepting the possibility of failure, acquiring an appetite for uncertified results, and viewing obstacles as opportunities to win are essential ingredients in the struggle for success. Listening to the ideas of others and being less analytical are also valuable pursuits. Banana thinkers comprehend that the number of chances taken are directly proportional to the number of successful endeavors.

> *...a high level of risk-taking enthusiasm is the key to increased prosperity.*

Intuitive risk taking can help maintain a level of excitement that you need to stay motivated. So trust your instincts and realize that maintaining a high level of risk-taking enthusiasm is the key to increased prosperity. If you sincerely want to lead a more effective and satisfying life, then throw away those secure analytical habits. It is only by risking yourself that you will experience genuine fulfillment.

CHAPTER 16

Stress Liberation

He plays, runs, eats, sleeps, pounds his chest, and yes, every once in a while he even laughs. Otto experiences life at the simplest of levels. He has no stress. He has no worries. His existence is full of satisfaction. He wants not, because he doesn't know all there is to want.

Here is yet another lesson from Otto. We need to get back to the basics with our lives. It is the complications of today's world that cause stress. It is our cars, houses, money, and jobs that are the root of the problem. We must learn to worry less about the material things of life and concentrate more on having fun, the health of our bodies, and living to be – not living to want.

> Is job stress literally killing you?

Today's business environment is breeding an ever-increasing stressed workforce. Most people take themselves and their work too seriously. They manage from one crisis to another and never have time to relax.

Is job stress literally killing you? Are you concerned about the level of happiness that you experience in your current employment? Are you in a sad state at the end of the workday? Do you return home a mere shell of a person? Are you mentally exhausted and so tense that you require a depressant to keep you from climbing the walls?

We need to get back to the basics with our lives.

Managing the stress in your life is necessary to remain productive. Providing your body with adequate sleep, relaxation, and anxiety relief is essential to leading a fulfilling life.

The seven major organizational stressors have been identified as interunit conflict, technical problems, efficiency problems, role frustration, staff shortages, short lead times, and too many meetings.[1] You are probably confronted with one or more of these stressors during each workday. So for your own salvation, you must find a way of effectively dealing with these difficulties.

A conservative estimate of the cost of stress is 10 percent of the United States gross national production,[2] which is presently in the hundreds of billions of dollars. Understandably, it is not a very realistic or desirable goal to eliminate stress totally from the workplace. But a high-stress environment tends to stunt creativity, hinder the motivation of employees, and inhibit the growth of an organization. One can just imagine what a small percentage increase in ingenuity or the caliber of judgment could do to boost organizational profits.

Sometime in the late 1970s and early 1980s, life and work became ultracomplicated. Over a period of a few short years we woke up to a highly competitive global business world. New things such as computers, mass marketing, and foreign competition began to entangle us in an ever-intensifying battle to beat the competition and succeed.

And things are only going to get worse. Look back at the changes that have taken place in the last ten years. During the next decade, the rate of change will be staggering. If you are having problems coping now, you can only imagine what you will experience in the not-too-distant future. You are going to have to change the way in which you work and play if you are to survive the next quantum leap in business progress.

> *Managing the stress in your life is necessary to remain productive.*

The costs of stress are also reflected in the quality of life. The strain placed on family relationships, friendships, and self are immense. If dollar amounts could be assigned to happiness, we would most certainly find that the aforementioned gross national product estimates are inconsequential.

You can live and work in a low-stress environment, but you must be proactive. You must create your own positive stress climate and make sure that it fits the organization in which you are currently employed.

Envision a business climate where you love your job, experience little negative stress during each workday, and look forward to a long and happy life. Wouldn't you be much more productive in such an environment?

> **"Serious work should be done for the sake of play."**
>
> — **Plato**

Find a new job or create an atmosphere in your present workplace where you can have fun and play. Just the word *work* has a negative connotation. Most people see work as a sacrifice – something that they really shouldn't enjoy. Therein lies the problem. Until everyone understands that work and play can be synonymous, our stressful environment will continue.

Work Smart, Not Hard

Major gains in productivity don't come from working harder, they come from working smarter. And play is a large part of the answer to the stress problem. It is what life was created for. Become too serious, and you lose the true meaning of life. Play too little, and you become a person only concerned with the means to an end, and all the while you will be enjoying life less than those who play more.

So rediscover the magic of playing. Find something that you like to do, and would do, for no other reason than your enjoyment. Incorporate it into your life. It must be so important that you would be less of a person without it. It must be such a part of you that your inner-self can't be separated from the nature of it. It must be fun, and you must be able to categorize it as play.

**"Methinks that the moment my legs begin
to move, my thoughts begin to flow."
— Henry David Thoreau**

There is a lack of meditation time spent in today's hustle and bustle world. People need to slow down once in a while, reflect on where they are headed, and confirm they are on the right track to attaining their goals. They also need to make sure there is enough of them left to enjoy success when they finally get there.

Running or brisk walking is a relaxation and meditation technique all rolled into one. Recent studies have shown that hard physical activity during leisure time results in a significant reduction in the risk factors associated with heart attack.[3] Exercise that is work is ineffectual, but regular exercise that is play will contribute to reduced stress buildup, good health, and a longer life.

If you are a habitual runner, you can sense the benefit of the activity. You can feel the strain leaving your body with each stride. After a run you have a sensation of tranquillity that is better than any drug or any other activity can provide. It is a primal thing that relieves the unrest inside of you.

Running may be the best exercise, and one of the best stress relievers, but it must come from within. Otherwise, do whatever aerobic exercise makes you feel the best. It should be something that you crave – something that gives you a feeling of fulfillment.

> **"Sleep that knits up the raveled sleeve**
> **of care,**
> **The death of each day's life, sore**
> **labor's bath,**
> **Balm of hurt minds, great nature's**
> **second course,**
> **Chief nourisher in life's feast."**
> **— William Shakespeare**

Sleep is nature's way of bodily rejuvenation after a long day's work and play. Adequate sleep is necessary to heal the stress wounds of the day. You must get enough of it to remain alert so that you can effectively deal with the many situations of life.

Think back for a moment to when you were a child. During the course of the day when you would literally wear yourself out playing, then after supper you would be physically and mentally fatigued. So you would go to bed at a reasonable hour and awaken the next morning refreshed and renewed.

Now that you are much older, you have become so busy in your work and personal life that you have forgotten the importance of a good night's sleep. You retire late every night and get up early in the morning not revitalized, but cranky and lethargic.

Sleep is an essential ingredient in the battle against stress. If you regularly get too little of it, you will be irritable during the workday. Every little problem will cause you to feel stressed. You will be angry with the very nature of your existence – and all because your body has not been satisfied with enough sleep.

> **"We must laugh before we are happy, for fear we die before we laugh at all."**
>
> — Jean de La Bruyère

Humor also lowers tension. Anyone who doesn't have a sense of humor is a candidate for stress-induced burnout. The person who has a humorous attitude toward life has the capability to be less judgmental concerning the practical aspect of most situations, and is better able to simply enjoy the differences that life has to offer. The serious person tends to be too absolute and earnest about future events. But the person with an elaborate sense of humor tends to be more relaxed, less disappointed by failure, and generally leads a happier life.

Laughter is an excellent stress reliever. The more you laugh, the better you feel. Laughter may very well be the body's best defense mechanism against stress buildup. It is okay to have a "laugh-at-anything attitude." In so doing you are preserving yourself. Those of us who laugh frequently and freely will accumulate less stress in our lives.

Anyone who doesn't have a sense of humor is a candidate for stress-induced burnout.

Type A behavior should also be considered. People who exhibit such behavior have proven to be at a higher risk of heart attack and other physical disorders.[4] It has also been verified that diet is not the sole method of regulating blood cholesterol levels. In many studies exercise and a positive attitude have been proven to reduce cholesterol levels.[5]

Type A people exhibit free-floating hostility toward other people.[6] This in itself is an indication of a high-stress lifestyle. If you are mad at the world, then how can you enjoy life? Accepting the differences of other people is the only way to cope in today's world. In so doing you will be decreasing your hostility toward others, and you will enjoy life more. You will also be positively affecting your health by diminishing stress and reducing your blood cholesterol level.

Sabbaticals are another way to reduce stress. When an organization gives its employees, "time off," it reaps rewards such as avoidance of stress-related burnout as well as increased loyalty and commitment.[7] The prime burnout candidate is the ambitious individual who can think about nothing else but success. Burnout is one of a company's worst competitors. If employees are burned out and lacking in motivation, profits will surely suffer.

With the inevitable "downsizing" of many of today's corporations, sabbaticals are a good way to keep people happy and actively involved. Companies should consider sending people on extended assignments to obtain additional formal education, self-education, to work as instructors in areas of expertise, or to serve charitable organizations.

Companies should do whatever is necessary to help reduce employee tension such as providing workout facilities or fitness club memberships. Establishing a fun atmosphere where play is synonymous with work and providing self-discovery seminars are also effective. Employees should also be encouraged to spend their vacation time doing something fun. The rest is up to the individual.

> *Don't be so serious. Enjoy what you have and reflect on your progress.*

So don't be so serious. Enjoy what you have and reflect on your progress. This is not to say that you shouldn't try to get more of everything. But in your striving to get more, don't lose part of yourself. Stress will do that to you. It will creep up on you in insignificant situations and turn your stomach inside out. It will cause you to doubt yourself. It will compel you to enjoy life less, and it will cut your life short.

Reducing the stress level in your life is essential to your happiness. If you want to enjoy a long, satisfying existence, then you must start now. So take action to save yourself from the dreadful effects of stress. The only thing you have to lose is the stress in your life. And on the road to discovery, you might gain the happiness that you have been missing.

Play more, exercise regularly, enjoy a sense of humor, get adequate rest, and accept the differences of others. You should also take sabbaticals when offered, and indulge in a long vacation at least once every year. The benefits you will reap from such endeavors will be reduced stress, increased performance and creativity, heightened job satisfaction, and added happiness. The benefits to your organization will be decreased health care costs, increased loyalty, and elevated profits.

By committing yourself to stress reduction, you will experience the miracle of rejuvenation, and you will lead a happier life. You can augment your existence and achieve all that you desire by taking the steps now to liberate yourself from stress.

A Deep Breathing Exercise

A chapter on stress relief would not be complete without a deep breathing exercise, so here is the one that I have devised for you. Take a deep breath and hold it for five seconds. Then let the breath exit very slowly through your mouth until you have almost totally evacuated your lungs. (This should take another ten seconds.) Return to normal breathing for about ten seconds, then repeat. If this cycle is repeated three to four times, then at least part of your tension due to stress should be relieved.

Use the above stress relief exercise whenever your day has been extremely stressful. The deep breathing exercise should help relieve tension in your chest, arms, legs, and other areas where your muscles constrict during a stressful period.

Now, remember for a second how Otto loves and lives his life on the simplest of levels. He knows that his survival is dependent upon the "successful daily operations" in that jungle he calls home. But he never gets too busy to play around a bit and laugh. So take another lesson from Otto. Quit taking life so seriously. You don't need the stress!

CHAPTER 17

Play As Much As You Can

So far our "bananas at play" discussion has included the subjects of baseball, persistence, risk taking, and stress liberation. But what do all of these things have in common with playing?

Baseball isn't too hard to figure out. And persistence is an integral part of any activity because it is necessary to practice persistently in order to excel. Also, risk-taking concepts can be used in a variety of games and different types of play. And stress liberation is one of the rudimentary benefits of play activities.

Play for Me Now

Play for me now,
So I can laugh,
And sing a song.

Play for me now,
So I can watch,
And string along.

Play for me now,
It's so much fun,
Living in the sun.

Play for me now,
Because I am so in need of frolic,
And being sedentary makes me sick.

Play for me now,
Before the darkness comes,
And I am whisked away.

Play for me now,
So I can play with you today.

The Opportunity to Play

There are instances to play that pass us by every day. What about that chance you had today to become a famous basketball player for just a moment, but instead you threw away a piece of paper with little thought of play? Or what about that chance to pretend you were a famous race car driver while driving to work this morning? What about that opportunity to take a longer pause to hear a songbird, or to merely stand and view the beauty of your city as you returned from lunch? Aren't such instances as much play as anything else?

What if we could play while we work?

What if we could play while we work? Some professions are viewed in this manner. Take for instance

218

a professional golfer. Could there be a better way to live your life than this? But what about all of that daily practice and the long periods that golf pros have to spend away from their families, and what about the strife to make the cut in every new tournament? I think that few of us could withstand the pressures of such a life. Only a few with real talent and determination do. That is why they are called *professional* golfers.

All professional athletes have similar problems. So do many other high-profile professionals such as movie actors, singers and dancers, TV media stars, and politicians, to name a few. They all have to deal with time constraints and the struggle to perform at their very best.

These public figures have to deal with the same basic problems that you and I do. They have to find a way to be happy while they work, and learn to play as they live. Some are lucky enough to end up in a position where play and work are not only synonymous, they are mandatory. But many take life too seriously, and even though they are supposed to be playing, they somehow never manage to have any fun. Still, the overall perception of playing while they work is true, because they work in professions that are inherently fun.

Why couldn't we adopt an attitude of play in our jobs? Why let the professional athletes, movie stars, and pop musicians have all of the perceived fun? We can whistle while we work just as well as they can.

219

Learn To Have Fun

Look for opportunities to play during your every-day job tasks. Then when you find avenues with which to have fun with your work, savor them like a baby tasting his or her first piece of peppermint candy.

Why couldn't we adopt an attitude of play in our jobs?

As we learned in the previous chapter on stress liberation, even serious work must be done for the sake of play. Play is very important. We work hard, perform our family and community duties, take time to improve and maintain ourselves, and all of this leaves very little time for play.

Often when people ask us to play, we decline, because we have "better things to do." But what are these "better things" everyone has to do that leaves so little time for play? Would you rather toil, drudge, strain, and struggle – or play? If you would rather roof your house or till the garden, then throw this book away now. This is not the banana way.

Pay someone to mow your lawn and play a round of golf or go fishing. Go to a movie instead of sweeping the carpet in your house for the fourth time this week. Ride the merry-go-round with your son when you take him to the park instead of just watching. Play cards with the neighbors instead of watching TV again tonight.

Get Involved

Don't sit and watch life pass you by. When you are spectating, you are living your life through

 220

others. But when you are actively participating in a game, you are truly living. A moderate amount of bystanding is appropriate and even soothing to the very active person. If your body needs rest, then spectating is an appropriate way to get it, but don't overdo it to the point of laziness. Those who spectate the majority of the time are missing the point of sports and play.

Games are there for us to test our skills. You can learn much more from a game if you play it rather than watch it. If you actually participate in playing a game, you have to do several things that a spectator often neglects.

First, you have to know the rules, and the better you know them, the more enjoyable the game. Second, you often have to put yourself at risk of losing. This in itself is an important part *Don't sit and watch life pass you by.* of playing. It is effective to learn how to fail and then find the strength to come back stronger and smarter the next time in a renewed effort to win. Some games have no winners or losers. These are the best games, because participants can concentrate on playing, rather than feeding their winning ego.

So Let's Play!

We are prisoners of our own choosing. We lock ourselves in and come out only to replenish our supplies. We must get out of our houses and experience the world. We must frolic with our bare feet in the

221

cool sand. We must swim the mighty waters of life to fulfill our greatest pursuits.

Many who spectate say they are doing so to relax. But I refer to such immobility as "rationalized laziness." People need to be active. It is good to get that heart pumping and the mind churning. Active play is food for the spirit.

Our lives must truly be lived for the sake of dynamic play. Until we can stand no more, we need to participate for fear we will decline before our deeds are done. Now is the time to be on our feet running, skiing, swimming, climbing, skating, walking, dodging, jumping – doing. We can lounge in our retirement, or better yet, in the grave.

We must stretch our wings if we are to touch the stars. We must truly experience the great outdoors if we are to accurately predict future trends in our world. We must take our drivers, bats, racquets and sticks to hit those extraordinary shots if we are to survive the onslaught of our aging bodies with any semblance of our past selves. We must cast our lures into the pools of lively frolic as we experience life to the fullest in active play.

Let us ride passionately into the sunset on a coal-black stallion, feeling the sting of the wind on our face as we catch the last few rays of sunlight before the darkness comes. When the night falls on our lives, what will it be that we wished we had done? Watch more, or do more? Do more, of course!

Think about the old man or woman telling how gloriously they played when they were young. Their bodies were capable of so much more then, and they relish the few experiences they can remember. How they wish they could climb one more mountain, or pedal a bicycle at high speed. Their best memories consist of those in which their lives were involved in the dynamic of frolic. If they played too little, their sorrow is great. If they had the opportunity to do it over again, they would live to play. And they would play vigorously and relentlessly, surely they would. The next time you have opportunity to visit with a senior citizen, ask them their story, give them an hour, and listen to them talk.

So experience the most from life by playing all that you can – whenever you can. Whether you are pulling in the mega-million bucks as the star of Speilburg's new extravaganza, or are making it happen in a mid-management cubicle at widget manufacturing, don't forget to play while you work! The alternative is to enter into the motionless void of the sedentary masses.

If you learn to savor your existence through perpetual play, you will be tasting life on its highest level. And your reward will be knowing that you have left nothing unplayed – that you have extracted the most that life has to offer.

PART IV

Peel That Banana Now!

CHAPTER 18

Peel That Banana Now!

It is always time to banana think. But the best time to do so is when you have tried everything else and are so frustrated that you are at your wit's end. This is when it's time to remember to look at the problem from the top and the bottom of the banana. An innovative idea is what is needed, and banana thinking is how to get there.

It isn't that a problem can't be solved, it's that you haven't yet come across the right approach. You must be willing to open your mind to the unconventional. And you have to respect the different ideas of others to build on them and create your own original notion. You have to be open to think of what hasn't been tried before, and therefore, what has *never* been done. You have to proactively generate your own original solution to the problem. This is the way of the banana thinker.

Being original isn't that hard. It won't take geniuses to invent our future. It will take thinkers such as you who aren't bound by convention to simply go forward in banana determination. Even the U.S. patent office allows a person to vary only a part of an invention in order to call it his own. There are

227

times when all that is needed is a tweak or a slight twist to come up with the solution to a perplexing problem. And then there are times when we have to get so far out of the box that it is hard to find our way back.

When conceiving new ideas, our dreams are as important as reality. But we must first have a vision before we can move toward a better tomorrow. So let us dream of such notions as solar energy, monorail trains, hydroponics, space stations and starships, long before we can achieve them. On a lesser scale, let us set our sights on the smaller improvements that can be made in our everyday lives. In making these seemingly insignificant changes, we start off a little better than we did yesterday, and before we realize it, we have become considerably more effective.

Some dreams are very hard to realize, and many take a large commitment. Take for example the dream of a college education – it isn't easily fulfilled. If we have no college credits, it takes at least four years to attain such a goal. But just imagine the sense of accomplishment and our new level of awareness after many years of sacrifice.

Many of our dreams won't come easy. They may require us to change from our uncomplicated environment to venture forth into new areas where our comfort level is lower than we ever thought possible. But change is necessary if we are to improve. We must make these kinds of personal sacrifices to achieve our potential.

If It Stinks, Change It

While recently touring a United Way agency for teenage parents, I saw a great poster. At the top of the poster were the words "BABY PHILOSOPHY" written in large bold letters. Below these words was a picture of a sweet baby in a diaper with a mischievous expression on his face. The caption below the baby's picture read, "If it stinks, change it."

My immediate reaction took my mind back to a recent experience during a vacation flight to Florida with my family. I remembered how much I enjoyed changing my eight-month-old son's *lethal* diaper in one of the three-foot square airplane lavatories. That was definitely a case of, "If it stinks, change it." But then I realized I had not grasped the true meaning of the poster. "If it stinks, change it," wasn't merely referring to diapers: it was referring to people, attitudes, work habits, organizations, and even basic lifestyles. It was analogous to saying, "If you want things to change, you have to do something." And it reflected the idea that, "If something good or bad happens to you, it's probably due to your own actions."

What I had stumbled upon was another definition for the word *proactive*. I quickly rephrased the caption in my mind to, "If it stinks, or doesn't quite smell right, or isn't effective, then I need to try to change it, and probably the best place to start is with my own performance."

I once again realized that we have to be proactive in every sense of the word. We have to make it

229

happen. If it doesn't work as well as it should, then we have to push hard to change it. And if we fixed something yesterday that still needs fixing, we have to try again, hopefully with a better outcome the second time around.

Change will be with us for the rest of our lives. And sometimes it is difficult to know what we can change and what we can't. Big ideas are an excellent way to change things on a large scale, but many of us can't see beyond the scope of our daily routines. It is the smaller changes that we can make in our everyday actions that make a real difference in our personal enjoyment. Choices to change smaller things will initially improve the success of our personal lives, and eventually lead to the betterment of our entire society. So let's continually banana look for those things within our scope of influence that can be changed for the better, then devote the majority of our time and thought to matters that we can effectively do something about.

> *Let's continually banana look for those things within our scope of influence that can be changed for the better...*

The basic point to be made here is that we have to embrace change. It is usually the simplest of concepts that holds the answer to life's difficult questions. Let's be strong advocates of the "make it happen instead of let it happen to us" philosophy. We are the creators, the proactors, and the answerers of our own questions.

The way of the banana will also look for ways to get more enjoyment out of life, operate more effectively, play longer, develop better concepts, and implement the improvements that we have conceived. True banana thinking will imagine and seek to change basic ideas that caused mediocrity in the past, so we can work and live more effectively in the future. We simply have to adopt the attitude of, "If it stinks, change it."

Reversionary Bananas

Now that you understand the way of the banana, and have most likely peeled a banana from the bottom, you need to be aware of an inevitable snare. Sometime in the not-too-distant future you will have the desire to revert to peeling a banana from the stem end. So be on the lookout to overcome this reversionary tendency at all costs.

During these coming times of great temptation, it will be that ingrained adolescent ignorance calling to you. And if you give in, you will be right back where you started, on a course for a life of mediocre idea generation.

It is human nature that people will normally revert to the easiest type of task. But sometimes what we perceive to be easiest, is merely the first way we were shown how to perform a task or to conceptualize a problem.

Take for example the banana concept. It is likely you have peeled banana's from the stem end for the majority of your life, and only recently learned the banana thinking way. However, for the next several months, possibly years, every time you pick up a banana, you will have the desire (for at least a split second) to peel it from the stem end. Again, it is only human nature to have this desire.

The desire is okay, but giving in to it is not. Even though you know that peeling the banana from the bottom is the most effective way to get to the fruit, the original manner in which you were taught is so ingrained that it may drive you back to your non-banana thinking days when you peeled from the stem end.

It will be the truly innovative thinkers among us who will resist this natural tendency to peel from the top and go steadfastly into the future peeling only from the bottom. Every time you peel, it will be a constant reminder of new and better things to accomplish. And it will be an ever-present symbol of the possibilities that await discovery through new, original thought. If we are to learn how to habitually think out of the box, we must never revert to the old ways once new ones are found. We must also show others the way by demonstrating our new-found ideas.

The way of the banana is universal. So show your children – show your family. Show people on elevators whose language you don't speak how to peel from the bottom of the banana, and they will smile in recognition. You will be amazed at the number of banana ideas that will cross your mind in the future that have gone unnoticed before. Banana thinking is for you, and you are now its champion.

But how many times in your life have you forgotten something once you had already learned it? I would guess there have been many such occasions. Remember the overeating example? About once a month we gorge ourselves because we forget how bad it feels to have food running out our ears and how disgusting we feel with a bloated stomach. This is a classic example of reversionary bananas. You have to resist the temptation to overeat if you want to feel good about yourself, stay healthy, or lose weight. And still, time after time you will sit down to an enormous meal to waddle away thirty-five minutes later with a stomach filled to capacity. And it is likely you will continue, unless you force yourself to think each time you sit down to eat.

> *Banana thinking is for you, and you are now its champion.*

Any time you decide to eat, please think about the future. You need to ask yourself, "If I do this on a regular basis, will it mean that I will eventually gain weight, and with that additional weight will I be depriving myself of a long and healthy life?" The majority of the time the answer will be yes. So if you think it through each time before putting food in your mouth, your efforts to lose or maintain weight will meet with great success.

There are many other occasions in your everyday life that require thought before action. You have to make an effort to remember how bad the service was the last time you purchased an item at your local ultra-discount store, and never return there again. You have to remember how many names were on the waiting list the last time you went out to eat at 7:00 P.M. and endeavor to schedule your dining safaris much earlier or later in the evening. And you have to recall the Golden Rule every time you have a chance to make a fast dollar at the expense of another human being.

You simply have to think before you act. In turn, you will be more effective. It is analogous to the "look before you leap" concept. It doesn't take much extra effort to look first before you leap. Especially if the consequences of leaping could land you in a less than desirable position with horse dung on your shoes. So look before you leap and think before you *do anything*.

> *There are unpeeled bananas all over this planet!*

You will have to summon all of your banana thinking intellect the next time you try to solve a problem. Never forget, from now on it is you against the conventional thinkers of this world. If you can get out of the box on a regular basis, you can develop uncommon foresight. You will be coming up with new ideas while others are busy rehashing old ones. You will be thinking universally, while the conventional thinkers are still pondering planetary.

There are wonders to conceive that no human being has ever imagined. There are unseen dimensions to transcend and new physical laws to discover. There are untold wonders about our earth that have yet to unfold. There are unpeeled bananas all over this planet! And only those who can see past convention, custom, common practice, and superstition will be able to get to the fruit. The great banana thinkers of the future will be in search of new ways to do things. They will be in search of undiscovered truth. Unfettered by self-imposed boundaries, they will be able to reach for the stars and pull down ideas that would make Einstein and Newton weep with admiration.

It is not that difficult to think out of the box. It's something that you ultimately have to do for yourself. You must break free from the lunacy and moronic behavior that is spawned by limited-thinking. Once you begin banana thinking, you will quickly discover that it is not only limited thinking that binds the banana way. You will find that banana thinking is also bound by people who seek to dominate others. When you do meet these people, you will want to be kind, in accordance with the Golden Rule, but continue to innovate with your unconventional thinking. Continue to ask why, and meet their conventional challenges with kindness, but don't let them distract you in their reversionary ways.

It is easy for others to control you when you don't ask why. It is easy for others to tell you what to do when you don't seek and question the wisdom of the ages. It is all too common to let another person's ideas govern your own. You have to pick your own path, ideas, morals, and principles. And you have to refrain from reverting to old, ineffective ways because of the wishes of others. You have to be true to yourself and to your family. And you have to think, or be enslaved by those who want to think for you.

It is a sin to not seek the truth, and you will never be a true banana thinker if you don't choose to pursue wisdom on an infinite scale. You have always possessed the ruler by which to measure it – the appraiser of truth, the free-thinking mind. And now you know how to use it. So use it for good and for progress. Be bold with your ideas. Dare to come up with outlandish notions, then seek to prove them. Display your zest for knowledge. Ponder the wonders of your existence and the expanses of the universe, and you will truly be a practitioner of banana thinking.

Otto the gorilla says goodbye, and he recommends that you peel your next banana from the bottom as a reminder of the unlimited ideas that await discovery. You have the resources and capability to think anew. So what are you waiting for? Take the lead in life. Be a banana thinker.

A Banana a Day

Please consider what you've read,
And keep on thinking free;
A banana a day is good for you,
Eat, and you will see.

236

So eat one often,
And peel it from the bottom;
To ensure that new ideas
Will not be forgotten.

NOTES

Chapter 1

[1]Written by the author and originally published in the July 1992 issue of *Quality Digest* magazine.

Chapter 2

[1]Written by the author and originally published in an edited version in the November 1992 issue of *Quality Digest* magazine.

[2]Arthur Koestler, *The Sleepwalkers* (London: ARKANA, 1989).

Chapter 4

[1]Carl Bode, Ed., *The Portable Thoreau* (New York: Penguin Books, 1975), "Walden (Economy)," pp. 258-333.

Chapter 5

[1]The Beatles, song "The End," from album "Abbey Road," London, 1969.

Chapter 7

[1]Gorilla behavior as a model for human behavior is based on information presented in the movie *Gorillas in the Mist* (Warner Brothers, 1988).

Chapter 8

[1]Written by the author and originally published in the March 1993 issue of *Quality Digest* magazine.

Chapter 9

[1]Written by the author and originally published in the November 1991 issue of *Quality Digest* magazine.

[2]Kevin Phillips, "The Collapse of the Middle Class," *New Perspectives Quarterly*, Fall 1990, pp. 41-43.

[3]Ayn Rand, *Atlas Shrugged* (New York: Random House, 1957).

[4]Aaron Bernstein, "So You Think You've Come a Long Way Baby?" *Business Week*, February 29, 1988, pp. 48-52.

[5]Ann E. LaForge, "Why Women Managers Quit Their Jobs," *Glamour*, December 1990, p. 112; Magaly Olivero, "How To Keep Your Top Guns on Your Team," *Working Woman*, October 1990, p. 35.

[6]See W. Norton Grubb and Robert H. Wilson, "Sources of

Increasing Inequality in Wages and Salaries, 1960-1980," *Monthly Labor Review*, April 1989, pp. 3-13.

[7]Stuart Weiss, "The Sad Saga of Variable Pay," *Business Month*, April 1990, pp. 74-77.

[8]Ted Holden, "Big Bucks Vs. a Job for Life: Why Top Talent Is Defecting," *Business Week*, January 9, 1989, p. 58; see William Keenan, Jr., "Is Your Sales Pay Plan Putting the Squeeze on Top Performers?" *Sales & Marketing Management*, January 1990, pp. 74-75.

Chapter 11
[1]Written by the author and originally published in an edited version in the April 1993 issue of *Quality Digest* magazine.

Chapter 12
[1]Written by the author and originally published in the October 1991 issue of *Quality Digest* magazine.

Chapter 13
[1]Miayamoto Musashi, *A Book of Five Rings (The Classic Guide to Strategy)*, translated by Victor Harris (New York: The Overlook Press, 1974).

Chapter 16
[1]See Saroj Parasuraman and Joseph A. Alutto, "An Examination of the Organizational Antecedents of Stressors at Work," *Academy of Management Journal*, 1981, Vol. 24, No. 1, p. 52.

[2]See John M. Ivancevich and Michael T. Matteson, *Stress and Work: A Managerial Perspective* (Glenview, IL: Scott, Foresman and Company, 1980), pp. 18-19.

[3]George A. Sheehan, *Running and Aging: The Total Experience* (New York: Simon and Schuster, 1978), pp. 71-83, 119-131, 221-231.

[4]See Meyer Friedman, M.D. and Diane Ulmer, R.N., M.S., *Treating Type A Behavior and Your Heart* (New York: Fawcett Crest, 1984).

[5]Ibid.

[6]Ibid.

[7]See Edmund L. Toomey and Joan M. Connor, "Employee Sabbaticals: Who Benefits and Why," *Personnel*, April 1988, p. 84.

About the Author

Mick Harrison is a degreed mechanical engineer who worked in a corporate setting for twenty years as a petroleum engineer, operations manager, and financial consultant. He is what he likes to call, a "seasoned risk taker."

An entrepreneur in the purist sense of the word, Mick is a former business owner with plans of owning others. His style of banana thinking has led him to write various magazine articles on the subject of innovation and organizational structure and this book.

To contact Mick Harrison, please write:

P. O. Box 55325
Tulsa, Oklahoma 74155

GRILLED BANANAS WITH CHOCOLATE FUDGE SAUCE

Peel four bananas from the bottom.

Slice bananas in half as if you were preparing a banana split.

Grill over a charcoal fire or gas burner for 8 minutes.

Flip bananas halfway through cooking time.

Be careful not to grill bananas too long. Grilled banana halves should still be somewhat firm.

Liquefy chocolate fudge sauce by placing in a microwave-safe bowl and warming in a microwave oven for 30 seconds. Place equal parts of banana halves in four bowls.

Spoon desired amount of melted chocolate fudge sauce over each portion of grilled bananas.

(Makes one baby gorilla serving, or four adult human servings.)

Serve and enjoy!

For additional copies of this book contact
your local book store.

Trade Life Books
P.O. Box 55325
Tulsa, Oklahoma

Other titles available from Trade Life Books

*How To Be The Woman Of Your Husband's
Dreams
And not his worst nightmare*

*How to Be The Man Of Your Wife's Dreams
And not her worst nightmare*

The Little Book Of Olympic Inspiration

Ditto Heads Little Instruction Book

Rymeo Series by Cyrano De Words-u-lac

A Mother's Love Is Made Up Of...

Diamond Dreams

It's Time Again To Skip A Birthday When...

Now I See Why Life Is Like An Olympic Dream

Trade Life Books

Peel

That

Banana

Now!